BETWEEN PUERTO RICO AND NEW YORK:
A LATINA PROFESSOR'S JOURNEY

Angela Reyes-Carrasquillo

Publications, Inc.

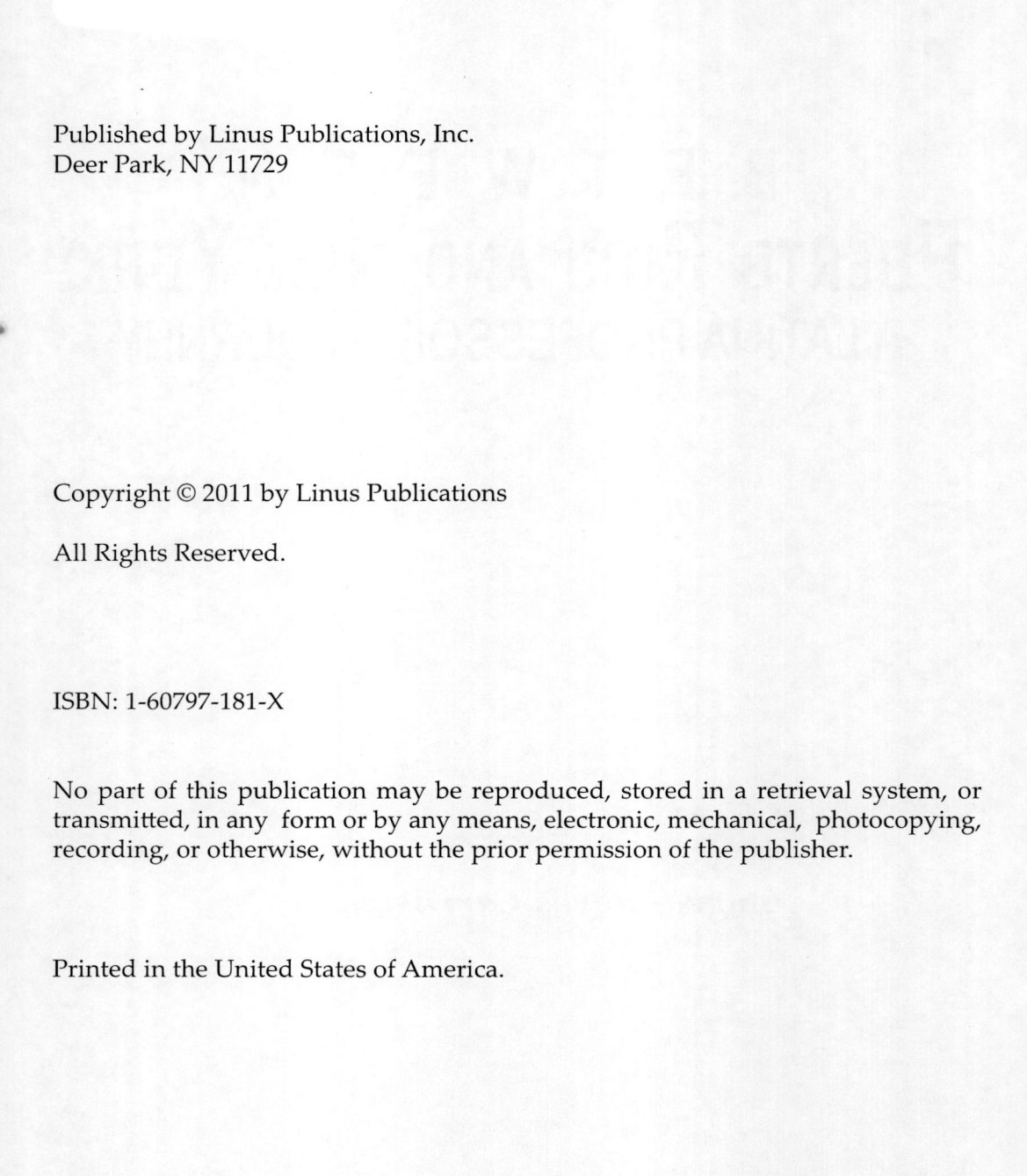

Published by Linus Publications, Inc.
Deer Park, NY 11729

Copyright © 2011 by Linus Publications

All Rights Reserved.

ISBN: 1-60797-181-X

No part of this publication may be reproduced, stored in a retrieval system, or transmitted, in any form or by any means, electronic, mechanical, photocopying, recording, or otherwise, without the prior permission of the publisher.

Printed in the United States of America.

Print Numbers   5   4   3   2   1

Contents

List of Poems v

List of Professors (Whose profiles appear in this book) vi

Dedication vii

Acknowledgements viii

Introduction ix

Chapter 01
Success is a Journey 01

Chapter 02
I am from Puerto Rico 09

Chapter 03
Growing Up 23

Chapter 04
Turning Points 39

Chapter 05
A Risky Decision 51

Chapter 06
One Day at a Time 69

Chapter 07
Being the Change 81

Chapter 08
Doors of Opportunity 97

Chapter 09
Puerto Rico in the Bronx 109

Chapter 10
Closing and Opening Circles...119

Chapter 11
The Intersection of Two Cultures 133

Chapter 12
Today is a Special Day...149

LIST OF POEMS

Puertorriqueñas: Women of the World

From Inside In

I Remember (L. Cortés)

Confesión de una Maestra

The City

You Will Not; You Cannot

Latina Professor

How Boring It Would Be!

Harding Park (M. Takahashi)

Single Women

Puertorra: ¿No hablas Español?

Praise the Day that Carries You Over (C. G. London)

PUERTO RICAN PROFESSORS
(Whose profiles appear in this book)

Sonia Nieto

Ana Celia Zentella

Diane Rodríguez

María Torres-Guzmán

Judith Ortiz Cofer

Linda I. Rosa-Lugo

Amarilis Hidalgo de Jesús

Alma Abdel-Moty

Magali Figueroa Sánchez

Aida A. Nevárez-La Torre

Xae Alicia Reyes

Nilda Soto- Ruiz

Milagros Marrero Díaz

DEDICATION

This book is dedicated to my daughter, Angeles Ivette and my two granddaughters, Alexis Bianca and Anyalis Iris. My daughter, Angeles Ivette was born in Puerto Rico; she grew up in New York City and currently lives in Florida. As a Puerto Rican woman with roots in Puerto Rico and New York City, she has experienced similar encounters as the ones discussed in this book, in her journey as a female Puerto Rican medical doctor. The struggles and strategies of her journey have affirmed her identity as a bilingual Puerto Rican woman and have, in many ways, opened doors of opportunity for her.

Alexis Bianca and Anyalis Iris are of a different Puerto Rican generation. Alexis Bianca was born in New York City, and has a Puerto Rican father and a Filipino mother. Alexis Bianca is presently living in Miami, Florida, and she shares her Puerto Rican roots with those of the Filipino and American cultures and languages. Her first language, English, is enriched by the Spanish and Filipino/Tagalog languages. Anyalis Iris was born in New York City, and resides in Clermont, Florida, with her two bilingual parents and a Spanish speaking *abuela* with whom she spent most of her early childhood years. Spanish and English are spoken at home, and Puerto Rican music, literature, and food are components of her daily life.

The doors of opportunity that my daughter and my two granddaughters have encountered, and will encounter, affirm who they are, embracing their heritage and its unique characteristics, attitudes, and attributes. I hope this book inspires them to be themselves, with their own beliefs and attitudes toward life and the experiences it brings, and to feel that although they have been raised within a diversity of cultures and languages, that they recognize that there have been distinctive contributions made by Puerto Rican culture and the Spanish language.

I want to acknowledge the role of my two sons, Olveen and Barney, and my three grandsons, Christopher, Andrew, and Angel in my life. I thank my daughters- in- law, Judy and Kenia, as well as Raul, my son-in-law, for being a source of motivation and encouragement for me. They, together with my daughter and two granddaughters, are my daily inspiration.

This book is also dedicated to all those individuals who have shared their lives in two languages and two cultures; and to those that, in spite of being born in the mainland United States, identify themselves as bi-cultural or multicultural, and who have had similar experiences within ethnic, linguistic, academic or professional communities as the ones narrated in this book. A special recognition goes to all those Latina teachers and professors who have struggled in two languages and two cultures, and who have had to deal very fiercely with unfairness and double standards in their search for equity and recognition.

ACKNOWLEDGEMENTS

I am grateful to the 13 Puerto Rican professors whose profiles are described throughout this book. Their stories are powerful messages of intelligence, motivation, dedication, perseverance, and firmness in their successful journeys as female Puerto Rican professors. It is my desire that more Latinas can share their stories.

I thank Lydia Cortés, Clement London, and Masaaki Takahashi for allowing me to include their poems. These poems compliment the message presented throughout the entire book.

Grateful thanks are given to Jane Ragno and Nitza Martínez, two dedicated and successful New York City teachers, who reviewed the initial manuscript and who provided useful insights. Their recommendations made these memoirs a better piece of writing.

I am grateful to Linus Publications for making the publication of this book a reality.

I also thank my *compañero*, Felipe for his understanding and patience while I spent nights and days compiling the manuscript.

INTRODUCTION

There are two main purposes in sharing my personal and professional life; a journey reflecting many spiritual, experiential, educational, philosophical, and academic experiences. One reason that motivated me to write this memoir is to describe how I was able to overcome poverty, prejudice, and traditional expectations for poor Puerto Rican women and become a "success" story. My story may send a message of "Sí se puede" (Yes, you can) to those with similar experiences. A second purpose is to narrate my academic life as a teacher and college professor with the hopes of motivating other Latina professors to share their professional stories and successes, to discuss their own struggles and doors of opportunity, even within communities of resistance. Latinas' voices must be louder than the voices of those that threaten their success.

I have been interested in the condition of women since I was an adolescent. When I was attending high school in Puerto Rico, I had the opportunity to look at the books and magazines available in the school library. There, I found the work of Alejandro Tapia y Rivera. Although he lived and wrote at the end of the 19th century, he is considered today to be one of the first and greatest Puerto Rican narrators due to his rich use of the Spanish language, as well as the messages sent through his writings. He wrote about topics and ideas that were not accepted and welcomed by the society and government of the time. One of his books that I remember reading was *Mis Memorias*, an autobiography. In this book, he wrote about the inhumane treatment of slaves, and about the rights of educating and schooling women (sensing that what he said could have been used against him or his family, he instructed that his memoirs be published after his death.). As an avid adolescent reader, the content and message of the book attracted me, and I tried to get other writings related to women's issues. At that time, there were very few writings on this topic. However, I found the magazine *Azucena*, and it too impacted me. This magazine was edited by Tapia y Rivera and his wife. The magazine published topics and themes about the condition of the women of Puerto Rico. *Mis Memorias* and *Azucena* contributed to my early interest in women's 'doors of opportunity.' Tapia y Rivera's writings provided me with information and reflections on the characteristics, conditions, needs, and challenges of women at the end of the nineteenth century. Interestingly, one century later, many of those conditions are still the same.

I continued my search for writers with similar ideas. I read several publications of Eugenio María de Hostos and Salvador Brau. These writers were also pioneers in advocating for the idea of the educational rights of women. Both of them felt that education prepares people, especially women, to think by themselves, and to develop initiatives for their own development, growth, and survival without being humiliated by men. Brau wrote:

> *"She is sentiment, educate her, and your dissemination of the truth will be more effective; make effective through the woman the redeemable dissemination and you will spread to all places the principles, and in each lip you will have words of truth;*

give us mothers that they can teach scientifically to their children, and they will give us a country that can obey in a satisfactory manner."

Hostos once wrote:

"Los hombres, que hacemos las leyes para nosotros, para el sexo masculino, para el sexo fuerte, a nuestro gusto, prescindiendo temerariamente de la mitad del género humano, nosotros somos responsables de los males que causa nuestra infracción de las leyes de la naturaleza."

Hostos and Brau were constant defenders of the equal rights of women, especially the right of an education, for professional, political, and societal opportunities. These male authors- Brau and Hostos- helped me to understand that for no reason, in many instances, women receive differentiated, unequal treatment in society.

In addition to the influences of these three Puerto Rican writers (Tapia y Rivera, Brau and Hostos), reading the works of the pioneer Latin American female writers helped me to understand the need to work hard and get the best possible education to find ways to express my own thinking and beliefs. I was enlightened by the literature of Latin American women, in which the cultural and literary expression of more than 20 sovereign countries is presented, manifesting unique struggles for independence and survival.

Since the 17th century, women have been writing literature, memoirs, letters, and essays; writing about their families, their economic hardships, their subjugation, and their identity. These women writers wrote about a diversity of topics, including folklore, food, indigence, abolitionism, and race. They wrote from the heart, whether it was poetry, prose, or memoir. Sor Juana Inés de la Cruz, a religious sister in the Convent in the Order of St. Jerome, was a pioneer and prolific writer of plays, poetry, and other meditative texts. Her writings are expressions of the desire to communicate with the outside world. Later on, women incrementally gained access to the writing world outside of religious contexts, and they wrote about a diversity of topics. Initially, they wrote under pseudonyms or anonymously, because from this position they were able to start the critique of their own status within heavily patriarchal societies. Clorinda Matto de Turner (Peru), Juana M. Gorriti (Argentina), Gertrudis Gómez de Avellaneda (Cuba), Delmira Agustini (Argentina), Julia Lopes Almeida (Brazil), Alfonsina Storni (Argentina), Juana de Ibarbourou (Uruguay), Gabriela Mistral (Chile), Clarice Lispector (Brazil), Rosario Castellanos (Mexico), Elena Poniatowska (Mexico), Victoria Ocampo (Argentina), Griselda Gambaro (Argentina), Luisa Valenzuela (Argentina), Isabel Allende (Chile), Cristina Peri Rossi (Uruguay), are brilliant minds who have been sending messages, especially to other women, through their writings.

I also became familiar with Puerto Rican writers such as Lola Rodríguez de Tio, Julia de Burgos, Concha Meléndez, Rosario Ferré, Meche Marchand, Nicholasa Mohr, Luisa Capetillo, Sandra María Esteves, Esmeralda Santiago, and Tina Casanova. What do they all have in common? All of these voices use their writings to motivate other individuals, especially women, including me, to not be silent and to share our own struggles and doors of opportunity.

I always wanted to write this book but writing it has been a very difficult process and task. In spite of having been a prolific writer, no other piece of writing has been as difficult to write as this one. I have been trying to write this book for three years, perhaps more than that. And, in spite of knowing what I wanted to say, I was never able to sit and put my thoughts together. I started writing in Spanish, and I stopped because I thought that addressing it to only Spanish-speaking readers only would limit the scope and audience, especially Latinos who were born or raised in the mainland United States, and who may not read in Spanish. I put the Spanish version aside, and I started writing it in English. Well, I stopped soon after because I felt the English language did not capture what I wanted to say. For months I felt that I had not found the language, although I had the context, the content, the audience, and the plan for writing the book.

I did not share this confusing linguistic dilemma with anyone for fear of not being understood. One thing was clear: I knew that I had to write these memoirs. I went back and forth from Spanish to English and from English to Spanish several times. I felt that although I was writing a story, it was not coming out as I was mentally processing it. And, after many hours of self-reflection, self-analysis and several outline drafts, I made the decision to use the English language to narrate and share my personal experiences, reflections, strategies, and doors of opportunity in my journey as a Puerto Rican/Latina, as a teacher, and as a female college professor.

I hope that my story will be read by a larger audience, including those who are bilingual, in English and Spanish, and those who only read English. I want to tell the story that as a Puerto Rican woman, and as a Puerto Rican professor, my life has not been easy, and that my voyage has been a constant and continuous struggle. However, strategies within communities of resistance provided me with the internal and external motivation, strength and power, to go forward, living and working in two languages, in two cultures and with individuals of different professional, academic, and personal insights and agendas. And, as Nemesio Canales said years ago: "*Una cosa es saber y otra cosa es poder. Y tan malo, sino peor, es no poder como no saber.*" [One thing is to know and another one is to be able to do it. And as bad as it is, probably worst is not to be able to do it as well as not to know it.]

The book mirrors the author's diverse emotions, attitudes, and beliefs regarding past experiences as well as thoughts related to conflict, faith, love, and hope. These memoirs are an attempt at self-understanding, which is indeed, the deepest way of expressing our own lives. My journey perhaps is similar to all those first, second, third and fourth generations of women and men who have struggled through life, especially in two/three languages and two/three cultures; individuals like me, living in a cultural middle, who are bonded to two languages and two cultures.

It has been said that bicultural and bilingual individuals are capable of being successful in the micro cultures in which they participate. These individuals can operate in two or more different and multiple cultures and are not threatened by a rejection of the primary cultural identification, in my case, the Puerto Rican cultural identity. On the contrary, one's cultural identity becomes more flexible, autonomous and stable, and one is able to recognize one's self as a member of different communities simultaneously; but the primary becomes stronger and steady.

Living, working, and learning in two languages and two cultures have enabled me to have multiple perspectives of the surrounding environment. It has also been said that those that speak more than one language and own more than one culture, are more sensitive and sympathetic, and more likely to have the skills to build bridges, to connect and understand people of different backgrounds.

In dedicating my story to my daughter, my two granddaughter,s and all Latinas, I assume that they represent this linguistic, ethnic, and cultural mix of Puerto Ricans/Latinas. This new generation will need to develop innovative strategies to open their own doors of opportunity in two languages and two cultures.

Each chapter of the memoirs is prefaced with a poem, which to some extent, relates to the content of the chapter. Most of the poems are my own, and three poems were written by individuals that I know and admire as poets of the soul. Some of the poems are written in Spanish, some are written in English, and one was written in Japanese, and translated into English by the author's wife. These poems are not necessarily about women, however, they present points of view reflected throughout the book. I wanted to include poems with multiple sentiments and diverse points of view. I hope that these poems and memoirs enrich readers' bilingualism, biculturalism, and biliteracy.

Each chapter ends with a brief profile of one of the following successful female Puerto Rican professors: Sonia Nieto, Ana Celia Zentella, Diane Rodríguez, María Torres-Guzmán, Judith Ortiz Cofer, Linda I. Rosa-Lugo, Amarilis Hidalgo de Jesús, Alma Abdel-Moty, Magali Figueroa Sánchez, Aida A. Nevárez-La Torre, Xae Alicia Reyes, Nilda Soto- Ruiz, and Milagros Marrero Díaz. The main reason for adding these stories of success is to alert the reader that my story is not unique; there are Puerto Rican/Latina professors out there with similar experiences. By including their profiles, I invite the reader to use these professors' stories to motivate young generations, particularly adolescents, to search for doors of opportunities. Adolescent girls, especially Latinas, will have access to a fountain of strategies when reading these Puerto Rican professors' profiles.

Although the book is written in English, Spanish words, phrases, and sentences or quotations are used throughout the book. Many are thoughts that come from the heart, and for this reason, they are channeled through my primary language, Spanish. In addition, I use Spanish to maintain the manuscript's bilingual, bicultural, and Puerto Rican flavor.

In writing down these experiences, in addition to struggling with the content and language of presentation, I also debated with myself over how I would sign my name as the author. When I was growing up, I was Angela Reyes; when I married, I became Angela Carrasquillo; and when I divorced, I had multiple names. I understood that with marriage, I lost my childhood name and, to some extent, my family identity. I allowed myself to eliminate my last name, for a name that was not mine. And, in order to adjust to that nebulous reality, I came up with another incoherent name to help my audience recognize both my childhood, and my academic names. 'Reyes-Carrasquillo' is a symbol of my past, my present, and my future.

My journey is presented in 12 chapters, each one surrounded by a cluster of experiences. And although these experiences are probably similar to other Puerto Rican/Latina women, especially professionals living in the Untied States, I have added my own reflections that the reader perhaps can consider when in a similar situation. In short, the purpose of sharing these personal and professional experiences is that after reading it, the reader feels motivated, *"con ganas"* (with a strong desire) to continue to overcome the struggles of his/her own voyage within communities of resistance. Oprah Winfrey had the same message when in 1993, in a commencement address to the graduates of the all-female Spellman College, she said:

Be a queen. Dare to be different. Be a pioneer. Be a leader. Be the kind of woman who in the face of adversity will continue to embrace life and walk fearlessly toward the challenge. Take it on! Be a truth seeker and rule your domain, whatever it is-your home, your office, your family-with a loving heart.

Be a queen. Be tender. Continue to give birth to new ideas and rejoice your womanhood...My prayer is that we will stop wasting time being mundane and mediocre...We are daughters of God-here to teach the world how to love...

It doesn't matter what you've been through, where you come from, who your parents are-nor your social or economic status. None of that matters. What matters is how you choose to love, how you choose to express that love through your work, through your family, through what you have to give to the world...

Be a queen. Own your power and your glory!

(Taken from Chicken Soup for the Woman's Soul, Health Communications, Inc, 1996, p.54-55)

The Unlikely Professor
Sonia Nieto

I was born and raised in Brooklyn, New York, where I lived in a fifth-floor walk-up apartment in a tenement building for the first ten years of my life, followed by another tenement building for a couple of years after that. The second of three children of working-class Puerto Rican parents who had a limited education (my mother went as far as tenth grade, and my father only to fourth), I was as unlikely a candidate for academia as anyone could imagine. And, yet, it was a path I imagined for myself when I was no older than 8 or 9 years old. Why I saw myself in this way is a mystery: there were no teachers in our family, and no one with a higher education except for two cousins who had recently arrived from Puerto Rico. I suppose that my teachers were my models. I wanted to be like them, to have my own classroom, to work with children, to write on the board, and, in general, to do all the cool things they did. And, somehow, I knew that if I wanted to become a teacher, I needed to go to college.

This remained my dream through high school, by which time we had moved to our first (and only) home, a modest two-family house in a lower middle-class neighborhood where, fortunately, we were assigned to an excellent public high school. It was a difficult place to be in many ways: a huge school of nearly 6,000 students, it was a very competitive place where everyone else seemed to know "the rules" (how to get into which classes, how to get extra help when needed, how to choose a college, and so on), while my sister and I were clueless. She and I were, as far as we could tell, two of only three Puerto Ricans at the school, and clearly not as well off as most of our classmates. Although at the time I felt marginalized and lonely, I am forever grateful that I was able to attend that school because I received a rigorous and excellent education there, something that would not have been possible if we had attended the ghetto school in our old neighborhood.

My sister Lydia, a year older than me, had not really thought about going to college until a guidance counselor told her she wasn't "college material." The guidance counselor's offhand comment became the impetus for Lydia to show the world that she could do it. I was glad for her, but worried for myself because I thought my long-time dream of attending college might be jeopardized if she too wanted to go to college. I didn't know how my parents – my father, the owner of a small *bodega*, and my mother, a housewife who also worked at the *bodega* – could afford to send both of us to college. In our family, there was no expectation that we would study beyond high school. Although they took a great interest in our education and admonished us to study hard and do well in school, given their own lack of experience with higher education, it was something my parents had not even dreamed about. Unlike children who assume they will be going to college, Lydia and I had to ask permission to attend. Imagine my nervousness, then, when a year after Lydia started college, it was my turn to ask. I still remember that night as if it were yesterday. I was anxious all day, composing my thoughts and my words. When I summoned my courage and asked, Papi said, "Haz lo que tengas que hacer para que te admiten, y haremos todo lo posible para pagar" ("Do what you need to in order to get in, and we'll do everything we can to pay for it"). I was ecstatic.

That was the beginning for me. Lydia and I attended St. John's University in Brooklyn, commuting every day by subway or bus. These were some of the most exhilarating and transformative years of our lives. After that, it was a graduate program in Spain right after college. When I returned, I began my teaching career in a junior high school in Brooklyn, followed by a teaching job at P.S. 25, the first bilingual school in the Northeast, and then four years later, I became a young faculty member in the Puerto Rican Studies Department at Brooklyn College. It was this experience that settled it for me; I decided that I wanted to dedicate my professional career to the preparation of teachers, something I did for 25 years after completing my doctoral degree a few years later. I have had an incredibly rewarding career teaching, researching, writing, and working as an advocate for social justice in education. But it was my parents' leap of faith in making a college education possible for us that gave Lydia (who went on to complete a master's degree in bilingual special education) and me the chance to dream of greater possibilities than they had been given.

Puertorriqueñas: Women of the World

These are the daughters of conscious, strong and clever people
their foremothers crossed oceans and survived nightmares
bringing multiethnic perspectives of three wonderful worlds
not just representing a cold, uncreative molded melting pot
but a mixed salad of attitudes, values, individualism and freedom.

Daughters of a land of unresolved political and linguistic issues
comfortable heritage of Taíno, African and Spanish blood
and carefully adding small and tiny pieces of the Anglo culture
unfortunately inheriting traces of unclear and unbalanced power
where contributions are mainly dependent upon male perceptions.

These powerful women would never try to culturally fit in
and they're fervently pushed by a wealth of pride and talents
showing multiple and universal values, uniqueness, distinction
balanced among sadness, sacrifices, diversity and spirituality
showing to be powerful in conviction and strong in adversity.

Because of internal and external imminent battles and reflections
they are pushers, the fiercest *luchadoras* and strongest women
diaspora, togetherness, dominance, wisdom and affirmation
racial/ethnic discrimination and prejudice prevent assimilation
historical competence, self-esteem and community consciousness.

Long lasting respect for education, commitment and achievement
totally involved in community, social and charitable activities
contributors of medicine, literature, arts, history and language
great educators, respected politicians and human law enforcers
moving even up to the unreachable federal Supreme Court.

They think of themselves not as a martyr or a *sirvienta*
challenging those in positions of power and networks
including priests, teachers, professors, bosses and husbands
some are single, housewives, partners or mere companions
single mom, foster mothers, aunties or childless by choice
they may be straight, lesbian, bi-sexual or just undecided.

They light candles to the *santos* and the many *virgencitas*
and have parties for their dead ancestors or powerful spirits
they leave grass to the three wise and generous three kings
who in turn leave toys, clothing or money under the bed
so, these women profess spirituality in a diversity of forms.

They embrace the cultural amalgam with joy and happiness
they flip from *salsa, merengue, reguetón* to hip hop or rock'n roll
enjoying the body cadence, the laughter *y con mucho gusto*
accepting themselves in their professional and personal success
emphasizing openly, publicly and proudly one's *puertorriqueñidad*.

XVIII

Chapter 1

SUCCESS IS A JOURNEY

I was sitting down at the kitchen table, the sunlight harsh against the small windowpane, when I saw the mailman putting the envelopes in the mailbox. As usual, I opened the door, took the mail and looked through all of the envelopes. I saw an envelope from the "Office of the President," and I began to read it:

> *"Distinguished professorships are among the very highest honors for intellectual achievement which a university can offer. Congratulations on your being named the Claudio Aquaviva Distinguished Professor of Education, an award which acknowledges your extraordinary accomplishment in each of the areas of scholarship, teaching and service."*

This letter was sent to me at the beginning of the month of September. And, although a tip was given to me that the announcement was coming, this letter really took me by surprise. In the past, I had received many promises that never materialized. But this was a fact, a reality, and it was a delicious and emotional surprise. This Puerto Rican *jibarita* made it to the top!

As I read the letter; I read it several times; and I paid attention to the entailments, to every word and the commas in between. And, suddenly, I thought that it would have been wonderful to communicate this great success with my father, that old man that had the bravery and strength to conceive me when he was in his seventies, who had profound conversations with me about God and the uncertain future of the soul, and who indirectly motivated me to push hard in life. I heard his voice and I heard my own deepening, as if my voice alone could rise against the chair to share this happy moment with that great man, my father, my first philosopher. Then, I began to mentally review the process used by colleagues and university administrators to rank and provide status to professors at colleges and universities.

Usually, college/university faculty is ranked into four levels: professors, associate professors, assistant professors, and instructors. Individuals move up through their professorship on their own scholarship, teaching, and service efforts. Being a 'full professor' is something that every faculty member in the academic world looks upon to achieve. The first step is to work extremely hard in the academic field in order to be recognized as an "expert." The second step is to get recognition as a scholar and the vote and recommendation of faculty peers, along with the blessing of several of the administrators involved in the process. It is a long and arduous process involving many ladders and many individuals who admire and value the individual professor's academic work.

A distinguished professorship is the optimal rank within the academic world. This rank is occasionally given by the president of the university to a handful of professors, perhaps one in each school, for extraordinary academic scholarship and merit. At the university level, to say that you are a "distinguished professor," is to say that your scholarship is recognized, not only nationally and internationally, but as one of the best in the entire academic community. At the individual's own academic institution, it is viewed as a powerful academic force, influencing the destiny of that institution and serving as a role model to the entire academic community.

I looked again at the letter. I read it in particular to the title I was given: '*Claudio Aquaviva Distinguished Professor.*'

"Who is Claudio Aquaviva?" I asked myself.

I went to my small office, turned on the computer, and clicked the Internet button to search through Google. What I found made me even more proud of myself and even more appreciative of the education that I received from my school teachers in Puerto Rico, especially from Mr. Díaz, one of my high school Spanish teachers.

I learned that Claudio Aquaviva was a Roman Catholic Jesuit priest who lived in Italy during the 16th century, and who became a powerful and well-respected religious and educational leader. Through his leadership, the Society of Jesus increased its members, its houses, and its provinces. Father Aquaviva's outstanding abilities included human, religious and educational wisdom, and extraordinary political ability; he was a great administrator, and a good transmitter and practitioner of the Jesuit philosophy. He is considered today as one of the founders of the Society of Jesus, and the father of the Jesuit system of education. What an extraordinary man!

I finished reading Father Aquaviva's biography on that tropical September Saturday, and I trembled to think that I had been bestowed with a distinguished professorship under Father Aquaviva's name. I was the first faculty member from my university to receive the Father Aquaviva's distinguished appointment. I was the second distinguished professor in the history of the Graduate School of Education. I felt humbled to receive such a distinction, but at the same time, I felt a heavy responsibility on my shoulders. Although I had a strong publication record, all those publications looked like very little in comparison to the work of the priest with whom I was bestowed a distinguished professorship. I felt like an ant standing in front of an elephant. I felt like "*muy poca cosa*" (a little thing). But at the same time, I felt extremely happy to receive this honor, especially when I was the only one selected from my school. Very few professors are privileged with this distinction. Most importantly, I felt that I was representing all the Latina professors working in colleges and universities in the United States.

I thought about what my other colleagues would have done, if they had received such a distinction. Well, if Professor John Smith would have received the Claudio Aquaviva distinguished professorship, perhaps he would have called another colleague, a college professor friend, and in detail, would have described the award and the reasons and virtues for receiving it. This friend, convinced of the merits of John Smith, and happy for Smith's academic recognition, would have written an e-mail, disseminating the good news to the entire academic community, saying something like this:

"This communication serves to inform of the wonderful news that John Smith has been appointed as the Claudio Aquaviva Distinguished Professor. Who better than our John Smith to receive this distinction! I cannot write here all the reasons why John Smith deserves this important appointment, but he is absolutely meritorious of this important honor. Please communicate with John Smith and congratulate him as soon as you can."

After that, I can imagine the procession of e-mails:

"Dear John; I am delighted to know that you were awarded this well- deserved distinction."

"John, I am so proud of you."

"John, your distinction is our distinction."

However, I did not call anyone. My Puerto Rican/Hispanic nature did not permit me to do that. I preferred that people knew by other means. I did not want to sound like I was better than my colleagues.

"I am sure that my colleagues will find out and will communicate with me," I thought.

I kept reading the letter, making sure that it was addressed to me and that the envelope had my correct Bronx address. I read my congratulatory letter again and again. But different from John Smith, I had no one to call and no one to congratulate me on the receiving of this letter and this appointment. My sisters in Puerto Rico did not know what a "distinguished professor" is, my children, the three of them, too busy in their own professional and personal lives, would probably have said, "Oh, Ma, that's cool! Great!" They were probably not surprised because they always think of their mom as a heroine and superwoman. And I am sure none of my colleagues were really interested in this benchmark in my professional life. My colleagues were too much involved in their narrow academic world. The only one who came to my mind was the Department's secretary; "she would be pleased and happy with this academic distinction." And, although she did not know enough about academic ranks, I felt the need to share it with her. "But not now," I thought. I would have to explain to her the meaning and significance of this distinction, and I was not prepared to do that just yet.

With the letter still in my hand, I began to see this distinction as a reality.

"I have come a long way, distinguished professor!" I said to myself.

I was still sitting in the kitchen, I folded the letter, and I could hear the birds in my garden, going around, down and out of a young tree that leaned near the fence.

"This is a huge, unbelievable accomplishment, and I have no one to really share it with," I thought.

Then, I stood up; I remembered that it was Saturday, that it was September, and that it was sunny, almost a tropical late summer. I went to the dining room, I took one of my most expensive glasses, poured some red wine, and I said:

"¡*Salud, negrita de Aguas Buenas*! (Cheers, small, dark woman from Aguas Buenas!) Well deserved! Wait until your colleagues know!"

The years that ended resurfaced and circled in my memory, and I returned to the present for the exact moment. I began to write reflecting on my journey as a Puerto Rican woman, as a Puerto Rican teacher, and as a professor. A journey that has been influenced by the challenges of my childhood and adolescence, by the many experiences as a teacher and professor in Puerto Rico and in the mainland United States, and by many struggles within communities of resistance. I invite the reader to join me in remembering and reflecting on these challenges and experiences.

La mujer es de la plaza, no sólo de la casa: Fighting for Linguistic Rights and Social Justice

Ana Celia Zentella

Growing up as the daughter of a hard working Puerto Rican mother and Mexican father in the South Bronx, Ana Celia Zentella's experiences in impoverished public schools and a crime riddled neighborhood alerted her to the significance of language and culture in the successful adaptation of immigrant families. Consequently, her research, community activism, mentoring, and teaching have heralded the varieties of Spanish and English spoken in barrios that are often marginalized and devalued. Bilingualism and multidialectalism connected her to 'hermanas/sistahs and hermanos/brothas' who taught her the most valuable lessons of her life, Phi Beta Kappa key notwithstanding. She met others like herself who succeeded in school without the support and guidance of caring teachers who could speak their language, literally and figuratively. Her perspective became international when she worked alongside teachers in a small town in Costa Rica, as a Peace Corps Volunteer. Back in NYC in the 1970s, Zentella was active in the Third World Women's Alliance (TWWA), working against the stigmatization of minority women's gender, race, and class. As director, playwright, and actress in TWWA's bilingual guerrilla theater group, she took skits that challenged sexism and racism to the streets of New York.

Zentella has shared the lessons she learned in her studies and community work with thousands of college students, first at Hunter College, where she taught for three decades in the Department of Black and Puerto Rican Studies, and then at the University of California at San Diego, in the Department of Ethnic Studies, where she became Professor Emerita in 2008. The Hunter College Latino Honor Society, which Zentella founded in 1994, continues to encourage students to excel and prepare for graduate school. Above all, Zentella's teaching and writing demonstrate her commitment to equity and justice. A recent email from a Native American student speaks more eloquently to her impact than any of her award letters: "Though you might not feel or see the changes that you have cried for in your books and classrooms, the motion has been set, and the ripples are now unstoppable." This student is one of 17 student contributors to *Multilingual San Diego: Portraits of Language Loss and Revitalization*, which Zentella edited in 2009, in keeping with her habit of providing students with opportunities to prove that excellence and diversity are synonymous.

Professor Zentella is known for insisting on a widely praised anthro-political approach to language, which unmasks the political objectives of language ideologies and policies. She is a preeminent figure in the study of U.S. Latino varieties of Spanish and English, language socialization, bilingualism, "Spanglish", and "English-only" laws. Her community ethnography, *Growing up Bilingual: Puerto Rican children in New York* (Blackwell, 1997), won the 1998 Book Award of the British

Association of Applied Linguistics and the 1999 Book Prize of the Association of Latina and Latino Anthropologists (U.S.). Her edited collection, *Building on Strength: Language and Literacy in Latino Families and Communities* (Teachers College Press, 2005) has been acclaimed by leading scholars and is widely used as a course text in the United States and Europe. Her latest research with "transfronterizos," students who have lived and studied in Tijuana and San Diego, breaks new ground by documenting bilingual practices and ideologies that challenge false notions about "ideal bilinguals," and "immigrant alien" discourses.

Professor Zentella has been honored on numerous occasions for her leadership on issues of language and social justice. In 1997, she was inducted into the Hunter College (CUNY) Hall of Fame, and in the same year she was honored by the Manhattan Borough President, Ruth Messinger, for her "leading role in building appreciation for language diversity and respect for language rights." In 2009-10, Ana Celia Zentella was named the Lang Visiting Professor for Issues in Social Change at Swarthmore College, PA.

From Inside In

I am here, sitting in this desolated park
alone, remembering my long and painful journey,
full of outside insecurity and inside confidence.
I was very much aware of my ethnic features
not too *flaca*, not *gorda*, not India, not too *negra*,
but with some combinations of the above.

I remember my tías and my cousins
always saying, telling me to stay out of the strong sun
because I was already dark enough,
a dark Latina, with a *chata* nose
making me aware of my skin complexion
but often lauded for my powerful brains.

I excelled in school, brains over beauty
a continuous war, fear and insecurity that I tried to hide,
progressive message of mainstream culture
not giving me an opportunity to report myself
pushing my own learning and my self-esteem,
only to be increased from the inside in.

I lived childhood, adolescence and adulthood
always thinking,
leaving the family nest for a path of my own
with a sentiment of pride and a lot of excitement
although recognizing and honoring my parents
the struggles they survived, and the era they grew up,
always from the inside in.

I am from Puerto Rico

I am Puerto Rican; I am from Puerto Rico. I am layers of history that speak of the acculturation of three groups- the Indian, the white European, and the African. I am made up of Indian freedom, Spanish colonization, African slavery, and American dependency. I come from a land of palm trees, beaches, rain forests, tropical weather, green mountains, *cotorras* (parrots), sugar cane, tobacco, and *café prieto* (black coffee). I was born in December, the start of the Christmas season, when the cool air brought way to the poinsettias and *azucenas*. In Puerto Rico, December is the month of *pasteles, lechón asado, coquito, and arroz con dulce*. This is a month of *parrandas*/music and family reunions. But rather than enjoying these 'delicacies,' I had been born.

I arrived that December, when the world was in a state of nervousness because of Japan's attack on Pearl Harbor in Hawaii, which at the time was a United States territory; an attack that left leaving thousands dead. The United States declared war against Japan and its allied countries, specifically Germany. Two days before this historical event, my senior citizen father, and my *treintona* mother, celebrated my birth in the beautiful cool weather and mountainous place of Aguas Buenas, a small rural town in the north central part of Puerto Rico. I was born as a result of the union of a man in his 70s and a woman in her 30s. My father, a widower with grown-up children, saw in my mother, a *jibarita* (country young woman), single and with several children of her own, an opportunity to start a new life and a new generation.

My parents were aware that there was a war going on; although due to the lack of radios or any other medium of communication, the information received was scarce and far from complete. But what my parents and other town people were very aware of was that many young men were leaving the tranquil town of Aguas Buenas. These youngsters were taken in the *públicos*, first to the *Campanento of Tortuguero* in *Cataño*, a US military base, and then, they were put in a plane to another military base in the mainland United States. And after a short training, these young men were sent to fight against the Germans and the Japanese. The people of Aguas Buenas saw many of the youngsters come back, but in coffins that were unopened, and with a soldier protecting the United States wooden box covered with an American flag. My parents knew about the human and financial consequences of the war because Puerto Rico was pushed to send many of their sons to the war. Perhaps my birth- that of a girl- was seen by my parents as a welcome invitation to resist a war that was imposed on the Puerto Rican people. In essence, my birth came in a year of sadness and loss to the people of Puerto Rico.

My family was composed of five members; my two parents and three daughters. I was the oldest. My mother spent her day doing the chores of the house, including walking half a mile to get drinking water from the mountain well. On Saturdays, she spent the whole day washing the family clothes at the nearby river. My father was too old to work, and had several ailments that did not allow him to go out often. We lived off the rent we collected from a small house that my father owned. Once a month, after receiving the $20 rent, my father went food shopping. That food had to last for the whole month until my father received the rent again. There was very little money left for anything else.

We lived in a very small house. It was made of a wooden frame with a cheap aluminum roof (*el sin*). It had one bedroom that barely accommodated two beds; one for my father and mother, and another bed for the three of us. The living room was small, no dining room, a small kitchen, and no bathroom- just an outside latrine. (Poor children did not have the commodities of the middle class or the rich.)

Coming from a poor family, and as a poor child, I had to help my parents with errands and house chores in order to help them to survive poverty and the inconveniences of a poor family. I lived most of my early childhood years in the rural area (Jagüeyes) of my hometown of Aguas Buenas, a mountainous *pueblo*. I walked about a mile to town two to three times a day to do errands for my parents or my neighbors: buy bread, stop at the post office, get over-the counter medicine, deliver a package or letter to someone, get a message to someone, return merchandise, or take someone to the doctor or hospital. I could not say "no." The word "no" did not exist in my vocabulary at that time. I had to obey the orders of my parents. I did not mind because that was the way of life. And, it gave me an opportunity to look at what was happening in this small *pueblo*, even if it wasn't much.

Illnesses were mainly ignored until you were very sick. One way of keeping illness away was by drinking the salty laxative (*salsosa*) two or three times during the year to eliminate the stomach worms. I will never forget my sister Maria with 3 or 4 stomach worms hanging from her behind. To make matters worse, we did not have any vaccinations except for the viruela. However, beyond the stomach worms, my sisters and I were three healthy girls. We did not get sick; perhaps a single cold that my mother cured with a plant bath that was blessed by our own urine. How we survived is beyond my comprehension.

Poor children did not have a lot of clothing. We had one set of school uniform -a skirt and a blouse that we wore the entire week of school. We had two pairs of panties that we wore the entire week: one to wear to school and another one to put on after coming home from school. After school, we changed into older clothing. Our clothing was washed on Saturday so that they could be worn again the following week.

I remember those years when we, the three sisters, were admiring the two or three dresses that my mother had. The material for these dresses was bought from the *quincallero*. At that time, *quincalleros*, a type of simple home supply seller, went through the countryside selling house and beauty aid supplies in their large *canastas* (baskets). Negrito, a 30-year-old single man (who probably was secretly gay) lived off the earnings of this difficult vending business. Negrito went to a different barrio every two or three weeks, stopping at every house to show his merchandise: hair combs, pins, hair cream, handkerchiefs, needles, face powder. If people wanted a particular product but they did not have the money, Negrito gave it to them *fiao* (without money), with the promise of paying him within the next two or three weeks. And when Negrito went back, some people did not even have the money. Negrito then had to wait again for several more weeks to receive the payment. I always enjoyed the visit of Negrito, and looking at all the things he carried in the canasta. Beyond the *quincallero*, we did not have any other opportunities to see merchandise for sale.

Three years passed, the war was still going on, and I was growing up. I remember my neighbors constantly telling me that I looked "*India..*" I began to ponder what being 'India' really meant. It probably meant that I had physical characteristics of the Taíno Indians: a *café con leche* skin tone, black eyes, black hair, and *trigueña*- not totally black but dark skin, and a small body completion. I began to believe that I was a descendant of the Taíno Indians; those men and women that by the end of the 15th and the beginning of the 16th centuries, went to the mountainous part of the island of Puerto Rico to escape from the cruelty of the Spaniards.

It was an early morning when the Taíno Indians were surprised by three *carabelas* (*tall ships*), cutting the profound waters of the Atlantic Ocean. Taínos looked at these three big birds, which were bringing many white, tall and bearded men.

"They are closer and closer," Taínos told the Cacique, their maximum government authority.

Suddenly, a white man, presumably the chief, together with a Catholic priest and a group of soldiers, were in front of them, showing their lances and swords, and carrying a big Catholic cross.

"Who are these people?" the soldiers asked the white man.

"They are Indians," the Spaniard chief responded.

Months later, a letter was sent to the Spanish Catholic Kings stating that:

"These Indians are smaller than us; they are dark brown with painted red and yellow bodies. They use necklaces made of seashells and rocks. Their hair and eyes are black."

The Indians who lived in Puerto Rico were from the Aruaca family and they spoke the Taíno language. Today, most writers simply call these Indians 'Taínos.' The Taínos migrated from South America, mainly from Colombia, Venezuela and Guyana to the Major Antilles- the big Caribbean islands. These Indians were pacific people although they resisted the attacks of other Indians, especially the Caribs who were extremely aggressive. The Taínos' main authority was the *Cacique*, who was in charge of the organization of the *yucayeque* (Indian farms), including the distribution of the vegetables, fruits, and sea food to the entire population. The Cacique wore a big golden necklace, identifying himself as the supreme authority. The second main authority was the Bohíque, the priest whose main role was to clean bad spirits and bad luck from the rest of the Taíno population. Taínos named the island *Borikén*.

Although the Taínos were not as developed as the Aztecs, Incas or Mayas, they did have a social and economic organizational system. They were acclaimed farmers, and they also created/invented their own sports and dances. One of the biggest social events of the tribe was the *areyto*, a combination of dance, singing and celebration, used to transmit the traditions and history of the tribe. In addition, Taínos showed great ability in weaving and pottery, they made arms such as the arch arrow, and the wooden sharp flint. They were mainly fishermen and they built their own canoes to go fishing off shore. They cultivated the land, planting mainly corn, *batata* (sweet potatoes), *ñames* (root vegetable), cassava, and plantains. Taíno women were primarily in charge of the agriculture, and the men were in charge of hunting and fishing.

Taínos, in general, were humanitarians and showed hospitality to strangers, lived simple lives, and had high spiritual and moral values. But the Taíno way of life was interrupted by the arrival of the Spanish. On arrival from Spain in 1508, Juan Ponce de León, decided to change the Taíno name of the island, *Borikén* to "San Juan Bautista," after a Catholic saint. It was customary for Spanish *conquistadores* to naming the conquered city with the name of a saint. That change of name motivated a young Taíno cacique- Agueybaná- to lead a revolution against the Spanish. This revolution lasted for several years. The Spaniards fought back, and after several battles, Agueybaná was killed in battle, and some Taínos hid in the mountains in the interior part of the island; others joined forces with the Caribs, and survived in Vieques, a small island in the eastern part of Puerto Rico. I am a descendant of one of those Taíno groups that hid in the caves and mountains of Aguas Buenas.

But in spite of the desire and emphasis the Spanish made to change all aspects of the island, the Taíno roots were never erased. For example, the original name of the island, Borikén or Borinquén, is alive today among Puerto Ricans. *Borincano, boricua, and borinqueño* are very popular adjectives used to identify and describe the people of Puerto Rico. The Puerto Rican national anthem, *La Borinqueña* sends a message of the "people's ancestral roots." Today, poetry, songs, literature, food, herbal practices, and language show that the Indian roots are alive, and that they represent an important part of Puerto Rican ancestry.

A few years later, the African traditions were added to the Indian and Spanish cultures. The Black, or African American culture, that mainly came to Puerto Rico with African slaves is reflected in many aspects of the island's ethnic composition. In Puerto Rico, African contributions are seen in the music, language, psychology, dance, and art. For about three centuries, these African slaves were brought to the island of Puerto Rico, and although, initially, they had an inferior status, they were successful in transmitting significant African cultural characteristics, especially sensual and rhythmic music imbued with spiritualism. Still today, Guayama, a city located in the southeastern part of Puerto Rico, is called *"ciudad de los brujos"* (the witch city), due to its continuous practice of spiritism and *santería*. The *bomba and the plena* dances are African contributions as well as the *baquiné* (a ceremony of the death of a child with music and songs). Cities such as Loíza and Carolina are still bastions of African descent. My curly hair and dark skin are reflections of my African ancestry. I believe my constant search for spiritual forces is also given to me by my African brothers and sisters.

By the end of the 15th century, Puerto Rico had become part of Spain. And for five centuries, Spain imposed a language, a religion, a political system, and a way of thinking on the island. Spanish influence is visible in all aspects of daily life in Puerto Rican society. For instance, Puerto Ricans speak Spanish all the time; the food is similar to that of Spain; and a large percentage of people are Catholic. Puerto Ricans are constantly proclaiming their pride in their Spanish roots. The fortress in San Juan heralded Spain's sovereignty, and the cathedral symbolized the triumph of the church over the 'primitive' Taínos.

It is fair to say that the psychology and personality of *"el puertorriqueño"* of today is the result of these three ethnic groups: from the Taíno Indians- the indolent character, lack of interest in material things, and hospitality; from the Africans- resistance, sensuality, and fatalism; and from the Spaniards- sublimity, devotion, and constancy. Growing up, I was not aware of the mixture of the Indian, Spanish, and African cultures. But later on, I learned that Puerto Ricans are not "one race" configuration; they are of a mixed racial heritage. Today, I understand why it is very difficult for Puerto Ricans to say "I am white," "I am black," "I am *morena*," or "I am Indian" because all of these terms indicate skin shades, types of hair, and other physical characteristics. Most of the time, when Puerto Ricans are asked what race they are, they just say "I am Puerto Rican," and that says it all. And, when Puerto Rican women are with their sisters from Latin America, they say, "I am a Latina from Puerto Rico." The Puerto Rican identity is more based on culture and language, rather than the color of the skin or the type of hair. Puerto Rican identity (not race) is a very powerful one; it describes an individual's history, ancestry, culture, and language roots, as well as the mixture of the three main racial groups.

For Puerto Ricans, learning to read and write was, and still is, an important goal. Parents wanted their children to become literate, although most children were sent only to primary school, usually up to fourth grade. My parents sent my two sisters and me to school mainly to learn to read and write, to "overcome economic and social disadvantages," thinking that through an education, individuals could rise from a humble household into fields of usefulness, well being, and prominence. And, with a lot of financial sacrifices and family restrictions, my sisters and I began first grade.

In spite of the simplicity of the school, evident in the lack of instructional materials, I learned a significant amount of history, learned to read and write in Spanish, and was able to do simple addition and subtraction, became familiar with Spanish writers, and was able to say, understand, and write simple phrases and sentences in English. I remember that in my first years in the public elementary school, all instruction was in Spanish, with one hour of English taught by the same teacher. English was taught as a subject, scheduled as part of the regular curriculum from the first year of school on. The use of the Spanish language as the main medium of instruction provided students with a sense of self-assurance, a sense of security, which later on became part of their Puerto Rican identity. The political status, difficulties associated with of rapid economic development, and the social and cultural changes of the island contributed to Puerto Ricans' ability to see language as a symbol of their cultural and linguistic identity.

Throughout my first experiences in school, I discovered that written symbols conveyed messages and dreams. I constantly read everything: labels on cans, old '*Imparciales*' (the people's newspaper), the "*munequitos*" or "*paquines*" (comic strips), and anything else that was printed. I learned to read in Spanish using the books *Corre Pinto Corre* and *Ana y Pepe*, popular early reading texts in the Puerto Rican public schools. Later on, I advanced to *A Viajar y a Gozar, and Libro Cuarto de Lectura*, my third and fourth grade reading texts. While in school, I would take books from my classroom, without permission, to read at home because reading them in my classroom was not enough. At the beginning, I felt a little bit guilty "borrowing" these books; but I felt I had to take them home. When I brought the book home, my mother usually asked me:

"Where did you get that book?" "*Me lo prestó la maestra*"(The teacher lent it to me), I said, knowing that it was not true, that I was lying in order to possess a whole book only for myself for one whole day. The next day, I brought the book back, hidden under my blouse or skirt, and when the teacher was not looking, I put it on the bookshelf along with the other books. That was my big secret, a secret that I did not share even with my own sisters. But those books, and the old newspapers I found in the garbage, gave me a sense of what life was all about. And, every evening, after finishing all my chores, I hid in a corner of the house or in the *batey* (yard) to enjoy the pleasure of a story being told to me through a book. Since I had very few friends in the neighborhood or at school, these reading materials became consistent communicators of friendship and knowledge.

The only friend that I remember from those elementary school years is Edna. We went to the fourth grade together. She was a middle class girl, who lived with her mother and stepfather. When I met her, her strong personality struck me, always showing an affirmation of who she was, without being arrogant. I observed her and talked to her several times, and because I came to admire her, I wanted to become her friend. Although she was the most affluent of the whole fourth grade class, which was mainly composed of poor children from the public housing projects or the near barrios, she was not haughty, and she shared with all of her classmates the candies she brought to the classroom. She spoke to everyone, and she smiled with a sense of humbleness. She had a friendly smile. I admired the way she was able to communicate a sense of friendship to everyone in the class. Although Edna's school uniform was of better quality than any other student, her hair was fashionably cut, and her vocabulary was rich and sophisticated, she did not ostentatiously flaunt of these middle class qualities. But I also noticed that she showed some level of sadness, reflected in her soft voice and sad smile, the cause of which I would learn about later.

I decided that I wanted to be her friend, and she accepted. We spent one year as friends, hanging out during school break. At lunch, rather than going to the lunchroom, I went with Edna to her nearby house, where I enjoyed ham and cheese sandwiches. She did tell me of the problems in her house and the cause of her sadness - her mother was living with a rich married man who spent some nights with her mother and the other nights with his wife. At the end of the fourth grade, Edna disappeared; no one knew what happened to her. Someone told me that Edna and her mother moved to the United States, perhaps to New York City, to start a new life. I missed her a lot; she was a great human being and a good *amiga*. Edna showed me the need to have *amigas*.

But let me go back to my early years, growing up in Aguas Buenas until I was seven or eight years old. I truly believed in the visit of the Three Kings, who brought clothing and toys to all children. It is the tradition that the Three Kings arrive before dawn on January 6th. For centuries, Puerto Rican children have celebrated *El Día de los Reyes* in the same manner as their grandparents did when they were children. January 6, the Epiphany, is traditionally the day in which the Magi arrived bearing gifts for the Christ child. I could hear *Los Reyes* opening the door of my house. I always wanted to go and welcome them, however, I was not completely awake, and I was afraid of getting lost. Also, my mother kept telling me that in order for them to leave me something, I had to be sleeping. So, on January 5th, I went back to sleep early, and I really concentrated on being asleep so that the Three Kings would leave a good gift for me. The next day, I checked the shoebox that I had left out on the night of the fifth of January, lined with green grass. I usually found something: a small plastic doll and one or two multicolored printed panties. I was always very happy with my presents, the doll in particular.

"I can now sew some dresses for my *muñequita* (small doll), but I will have to get the fabric from my mother's clothes," I said to myself. "If she finds that I am using these old dresses of hers, she will be very angry at me."

I remember that one year because I was the oldest of the three sisters, my mother wanted to reward me for being the oldest. So, the Three Kings decided to leave me a ceramic doll. I found this small, but beautiful doll in my shoebox. I was so happy with my doll! I did not stop playing and talking to my doll. But on the same Three Kings Day, while I played with the small ceramic doll, I dropped it. It hit the floor and broke. I remember the scene- I cried until I could not cry anymore. I tried to glue the parts together but they were so tiny that I could not do it. I looked at my two sisters playing with their plastic dolls, and I envied them. And, suddenly, I thought of a brilliant idea:

"Since the Three Kings have to go back to that far land from where they came from, and since they have to pass by my house on their way back, especially during the night, I will put back the shoebox with grass."

I was sure that they still had some dolls left, even if it was the one made of plastic. I went out and got the grass; I got *yerba de bejuco de puerco* with its beautiful pink flowers, like silk, and I put the box under my bed. I put a lot of flowers in it, for I wanted the Kings' camels to eat a lot and be happy. I told my mother my plan; I told her that I was going to go to sleep very early because I did not want to take any chances. My mother did not make any comments, and she left. I see in her action that to some extent, she supported my decision. I was sure that I would get another doll.

The next day, I looked under my bed and did not like what I saw. I found the box, still filled with grass; the flowers were still there, although they were wilted and dead. There was no doll. I did not say anything to my mother, and she did not ask or say anything to me, either. My sisters were too busy playing with their own dolls. I did not like the trick that my Three Kings played on me. Or, I thought- "they might have run out of dolls."

But there were occasions when the Three Kings did not get to my house at all, and no gifts were left in the shoeboxes. And, when the Three Kings did not arrive at my house, they also did not go to my cousins,' nephews,' nieces' or friends' houses. I thought the reason was that they, the Three Kings, could not get to our remote barrios because of the lack of roads and the poor state of the ones we had. We accepted the idea that the Three Kings were not coming to our homes; however, we had the hope of getting a toy from the rich houses located not far from our poor *chozas*. We were sure that there were gifts in the rich houses because they had money to give to the Three Kings, and also because they were next to the roads. Most importantly, these people had money to buy toys for us, the poor children of the *barrio*.

These mansions were the second homes or country homes for rich Puerto Ricans, especially the lawyers, doctors, and successful business people of San Juan. My father once told me that these rich people bought the land for pennies from *campesinos* (poor people). These rich people kept pushing *Papi, Abuela Mai,* and *Tío Justo* out, and into the mountainous areas of the rural barrio. My father recognized that he was one of those *campesinos* who sold his beautiful land for few dollars to rich professionals from the city of lights- San Juan and Rio Piedras. Their houses were built in the best part of the barrio, usually on a hill with an ample view of San Juan, the San Juan Bay, and Santurce.

The children of the *barrio*, including myself, thought that these rich families would give us toys. And, on Three Kings Day, about 10 children, including my two sisters and I went and parked ourselves in front of one of the houses where we could see people inside. And for about one hour we made noise and waited, and waited. After one hour of not seeing any distribution of toys, we decided to go to the next house, only to get the same result. Once in a while, someone dropped three or four small cheap toys: *a cuica, a yoyo,* and a handkerchief, not enough for everyone. But most of the time, we spent the whole day waiting for about four hours with no luck. Then, we returned to our homes, hungry, thirsty, dirty, and with no toys. However, we never lost hope. We thought that the next year there would be a better Three Kings Day. For the moment, we concentrated on the thought of going to school the following week. In Puerto Rico, school resumed on the second or third week of January.

During my early childhood years, Puerto Ricans were celebrating the opportunity to vote and elect the island's first governor. Luis Munoz Marín, the son of a Puerto Rican US Congress representative studied law at Georgetown University, but left college to go to New York City to become a poet and a writer. He established himself in the Lower East Side of New York, and frequently visited the Lower West Side of Manhattan, where poets and all types of artists congregated. He interacted with Puerto Ricans in the Village and on Orchard Street, particularly with newspaper journalists who made him aware of the political situation of the island: children being educated in English, having a United States appointed governor, and a powerless, non-voting congressional representative in Washington. This sense of communicating with Puerto Ricans and writers called Luis Munoz Marín to become involved in the politics of the island. While in New York City, Munoz Marín criticized the United States' dominance over Puerto Rico, and he supported independence of the island from the United States; although, he rejected ideas of armed rebellion. He went back to Puerto Rico and immediately founded a new political party, the *Partido Popular Democrático*, which emphasized dependency to the US but with political autonomy to the island. At that time, the 1940s, Puerto Ricans were struggling against poverty and financial hardships, and they saw Munoz Marín as their only hope. In 1947, when Congress allowed

Island residents to elect a governor; Munoz Marín was an easy winner. He became the first governor of the island to be elected by the Puerto Rican people.

When he took office, Luis Munoz Marín found a bad economy and a high level of poverty on the island of Puerto Rico. There were no jobs, agriculture was not producing enough to be cost effective, and factories and other means of production were non-existent. Puerto Ricans migrated to New York City in large waves, encouraged by the *Partido Popular* government, using the Liberty ships, (built to carry troops during the war) or recycled warplanes. My parents probably heard about the "good life of Nueva York" communicated by Puerto Ricans already on the mainland. Puerto Ricans wrote: "I live very well here in New York!" "I have a very good job!" "I make a lot of money." "I have water and electricity in my apartment!" "I go to the corner, and I can take the bus, or the train which will take me everywhere I want to go." These statements were common in the letters sent by Puerto Ricans living on the mainland to their relatives and friends back in Puerto Rico. Puerto Ricans in Puerto Rico believed that life in United States was easy, and that jobs and money were easily available. Once or twice a year, they sent a small amount of money and boxes containing clothing, shoes, and food to their family members still residing on the island.

My *Abuelita Mai*, (my grandmother), a poor single *anciana*, who lived in the remote barrio of *Jagüeyes* during the 1940s received a big box with a New York City address on it. It was a big deal to receive a large package like the ones sent to *Mai*. I remember that once a rumor was spread that a package from New York was coming, there were a lot of expectations by relatives close to *Abuelita Mai*. When the big box package arrived, all *Abuelita*'s daughters, sons, and grandchildren surrounded her to watch her open this big box. She took the necessary time when opening it, showing and displaying its contents: used high heel shoes, big and long dresses and skirts, used men's pants, used sweaters, and one or two packages of hard candies. None of these rare pieces fit me, and I wondered what types of people owned them. The shoes were too big, and the high heels were not for the hills of Aguas Buenas; none of the dresses fit *Abuelita Mai or* her daughters. The dresses were too long and the shirts were too big. I always asked myself: "Why were the people in New York not sending new things with the right size and height?" And, after the excitement of opening the box, and noticing that its content did not fit any of us, our daily lives of struggle and hope continued.

A Tenacious Advocate for Appropriate Education for English Language Learners

Diane Rodríguez

Professor Diane Rodríguez has often been referred to as *"a tenacious advocate for appropriate education for English Language Learners,"* a title she has earned throughout years of defending the rights of Latino children and youth. Her research interests encompass the areas of teaching culturally and linguistically diverse students with and without disabilities, multicultural education, and teacher preparation. These interests emerged when she was recruited in Puerto Rico to be a teacher in New York City. She witnessed the educational inequality of many English language learners in the public school system, and decided to speak on behalf of these children.

Professor Rodríguez completed her primary and secondary school in the public schools of Puerto Rico, where she was a second language learner. Professor Rodriguez graduated from the Universidad Interamericana of Puerto Rico with a baccalaureate in Language Arts. Two years after teaching English as a second language to middle school students, she realized that she wanted to continue her graduate studies. That is when she read an ad in the Sunday paper urging teachers to apply to the New York Public Schools to teach in various critical shortage areas. She moved to New York City and started teaching bilingual special education.

Professor Rodríguez attended the Graduate Program at Fordham University, completing masters' and doctorate degrees in the area of Language, Learning, and Literacy. She then continued her post-doctoral studies at the University of Virginia in the area of special education. While at Fordham University, she was nominated and selected to be a "Holmes Scholar," a national award meant to prepare graduate students of underrepresented groups in the education professorate.

In New York, Professor Rodriguez's advocacy role brought her to develop workshops to integrate mathematics and science into the bilingual special education classroom. She developed staff training workshops in the Superintendent's Office for many teachers who needed to learn how to more effectively instruct students with disabilities. During this time, she joined *Latino Children Educational Network* (ENLACE), a not-for-profit organization that advocated the promotion of bilingualism and biculturalism. She moved to Florida where she continued to work with educators in preparing them with the necessary tools to teach English language learners. Presently, Professor Rodríguez lives in North Carolina and her work as a tenacious advocate has not stopped. She is an associate professor at East Carolina University in the College of Education, Department of Curriculum and Instruction. She is active with the Association of Mexican Americans in North Carolina (AMEXCAN), whose primary purpose is to facilitate the integration of Mexicans and Latinos in their respective communities, as well as to establish and reinforce ties between the Mexican and Latino people and other communities in North Carolina.

Professor Rodríguez has received several grants from the U. S. Office of Special Education and Rehabilitation Services, and the Office of English Language Acquisition. Professor Rodriguez' publications include: *Freedom from Social Isolation for Young Students with Disabilities; Increasing Online Interaction in Rural Special Education Teacher Preparation Program; Understanding the Complexity of Special Education in Guatemala; Culturally and Linguistically Diverse Students with Autism, Meeting the Needs of English Language Learners with Disabilities in Urban Settings,* and, *Academic Factors Indicating Successful Programs for English Language Learners.* She is a frequent speaker at national and international conferences on special education and bilingual education.

I Remember
Lydia Cortes

I remember kindergarten

I remember having to say good-bye to Mami crying

I remember not understanding the teacher
The English lessons with pretty Miss Powell
who made the boxy words fit just right in my mouth no pain
I remember the teachers who said, *"You don't look Puerto Rican"*
expecting to hear me say thank you very much
I remember overhearing some saying *Puerto Ricans*
don't care about their children, Puerto Ricans aren't clean

I remember the heat of shame rising in my face
praying no one had heard what the teachers said, or
see my hurt red as a broken heart

I remember Mr. Seidman in the 4th grade and how he chose
me for a big part in the school play
I remember feeling important
memorizing my lines and Mami helping me
both Mr. Seidman and Mami smiling, proud,
the night of the performance. Looking at me!
I remember the audience laughing and...the applause
I remember moving to Flatbush from Fort Greene
going from a 5th floor tenement walk-up to
our very own private house on a quiet tree-lined street
I thought we had moved to the country
I remember going from Girls' High to Erasmus Hall

and how I went from smart to borderline in one day
Miss Nash, the bio teacher, called me stupid
because I didn't know how to use a microscope

I remember Mr. and Mrs. Hamburger – hamburger?
how I laughed at that name, when I heard I was getting
one for political science and the other for economics
I remember being amazed when learning became
a wonder-filled adventure

the faith each of them had in me
I worked hard for them both
I remember the A's I got in their classes

I remember being Puerto Rican in Erasmus Hall High School because
I was the only one - until my sister followed next year - on the academic track
I remember the guidance counselor advising me to become
a bilingual secretary since I certainly was not college material

I remember Papi, with his third grade education, saying,
"Lidin, tu puedes hacer lo que quieres. Yo te apoyo en todo. Siempre."

Chapter 3

GROWING UP

It was the beginning months of my fifth grade year, and for unclear reasons, I did not have friends in the neighborhood or in school. Loneliness took me to become friendly with a neighboring couple who had no children, Dona Fela and Don Santos. I went to this couple's home often to help with the errands of the house, and in return, they fed me and showed me affection. A couple of months later my parents announced that they were moving to a farther rural part of Aguas Buenas. During those days, I conveyed to Fela and Santos the sad news of having to change my school and lose my schooling.

"I really like my school very, very much," I said.

They offered me their hospitality, invited me to move into their house so that I could continue attending the same school. My parents agreed, and two weeks later, I was installed in their house. The transition was not easy; I found that Fela was very authoritarian, and I crashed with her several times. The house was small and there was no space, nor was there an extra bed for me to sleep on. I slept in a hammock which I frequently wet during the night. I hid this from Fela for fear of being reprimanded or punished. The next day, I had to sleep in the same stinking wet hammock. Fela never discovered my secret (or did not show it). I suffered every night, and I silently cried, and I did not tell anyone of my miseries on the hammock. What more, I had to walk to town several times a day to do errands; I had to clean the house, wash the dishes several times a day, and I had to take the frequent Fela's *cocotazos* (head hitting) when things were not done well. Confronting those wet and smelly nights gave me the opportunity to think deeply and become strong. I knew that, in my life, there were going to be similar nights, and I needed to be strong. One of the strategies that I used was to get up every day thinking that the present day was going to be better than the previous one. It worked, after one month, I stopped wetting the hammock, and I started to mentally adjust to Fela's many demands. I did not contradict her, nor did I share with her my difficulties. I used my little free time to read and daydream for a better life.

I went to Fela's house without a religious affiliation. My parents never taught me to pray or read any religious literature, and they did not teach me any religion. I heard that I was baptized when I became ill once because my parents were afraid of me dying *mora* (not baptized). It was only when I came to Fela's house that I became aware of different types of religions, the first one being *spiritism*. Fela used to visit Don Tito, a well-known *espiritista* (spiritist) in my town of Aguas Buenas. Fela and her husband, Santos, went to spiritual sessions once a week, usually at night, while I waited in Don Tito's living room. The sessions were held inside a room that I imagined was Don Tito's bedroom, or some kind of a sacred room. I sat there and wondered what was going on inside that room. I was not allowed to see or hear what was going on, but I always heard strong loud voices for a time, and then silence. And after that, 20 to 25 minutes later, Fela, Santo and Don Tito would come out without saying a word. I never questioned Fela about these meetings but I always knew that there were spirits that spoke through Don Tito. And somehow, Don Tito knew how to speak to, fight, and control the bad spirits. At home, I smelled the oils and leaves given to Fela by Don Tito, and I guessed that these herbs and oils had powerful magical powers. When I saw him in the streets of my little town of Aguas Buenas, I tried to read his face, surrounded by mysteries, and hidden under his military hat. I wanted to talk to him, and I looked at his face but he never acknowledged my presence. In fact, I never talked to Don Tito. When I went to his house, he always treated me as I did not exist, never even said *"Hola"* to me. I wanted to tell him that I was not afraid of him that I was sufficiently strong to know the intimacies of the soul, to deal with the evil and the good. And, while growing up, thoughts of Don Tito's were always with me. Why was he so strange? What mysteries did he hide?

None of the books I had read told me about these things. When other people from the neighborhood talked about *spiritism*, they looked at us, the children, and asked us to leave the room. But those mysterious events fascinated me more than Santo, Fela, or Don Tito could imagine! The experience of Don Tito helped me to reaffirm the need to look for something beyond the daily routine of going to school and helping Fela with the daily errands. I was hungry for knowledge and hungry for knowing what was beyond our soul. For this reason, I kept reading everything, every printed material that I found in front of me.

Several months passed, and Fela and Santo did not visit Don Tito again. And I did not hear them say anything about visiting Don Tito. His presence and teachings completely disappeared. And I did not have enough *confianza* (confidence) to ask Fela about what happened between her and Don Tito. Later on, I read that the first Puerto Rican *espirtistas* were Taínos. Yukiyú was the good god, and this god defended the land, the crops, the people, and the animals. The *alondra* (lark) always sang for Yuquiyú, and flowers opened to offer him their scent and their beauty. Similar to the *espiritista* of today, the best crops were given to Yukiyú. Taínos believed that there was life after death, and that when the Cacique died, he went to the *más allá*, (world beyond), and that the gods protected all those brave and good individuals. The Bohique, the priest, was the first Puerto Rican healer. With his words and his hands and a cold bath, he was able to retire the bad spirits and the illness from the Taínos that requested his services.

Fela decided to abandon *espiritismo* and embrace Catholicism. She became so dedicated to Catholicism that she went to church almost every day. I accompanied Fela to mass every Sunday and sometimes during the week, too. On occasion, I went to mass by myself very early in the morning. During the two years that I lived with Fela, she motivated me to go to mass as frequently as possible, and I usually went alone to the 6 AM mass. I woke up and, dressed and alone, left the house for mass. I lived in the outskirts of town and I had to walk about a mile to get to the town's church.

One night, I woke up, I got up, and I dressed, then opened the door and began to walk to town. I noticed that it was still dark but I did not pay too much attention to it since I always went to church when it was still dark. I noticed that the road was completely empty; no cars were passing by, and there were only about two houses on the road going toward the town. I began walking alone toward the church and half way there, a small passenger bus, a *publico*, stopped. I recognized the driver whose name was *Paquín*, who said to me:

"Negrita, ¿para dónde vas a esta hora? " (Where are you going at this hour?), he asked.

"Voy para la iglesia" (I am going to church), I said.

"Muchacha, son las tres de la mañana. Móntate que te voy a regresar a tu casa." (Hey kid, it is only 3 AM, get in, I will take you to your house.)

He drove me back to the house. Fela and her husband were sleeping and they did not hear me coming back and going to my *hamaca* (hammock). It never crossed my mind the dangers of a pre-teenager walking alone during the night on a solitary road.

Two years after being at Fela and Santo's house, destiny put me in contact with the English language. I was attending sixth grade in a public school, and Fela thought that it would be a good idea to send me to a Catholic school, to be educated by the Holy Cross nuns. Fela did not like to see me reading all those 'strange books' assigned to me in the public school, and she thought that in Catholic school, the nuns would be more careful with the quality of books I needed to read. She usually said:

"Angeles, I hope that you do not believe everything that you read. Be careful with those *novelas*. I do not want you to read those books."

But I read *Marianela* by Benito Pérez Galdós under a *quinqué* (gas lamp), hiding from Fela and her husband. She assumed that the best schooling for me was from a Catholic parochial school. Fela spoke with the nuns who said that before registering in the school, I needed to attend a summer tutoring program given by a retired teacher who volunteered to teach the new group of students. Fela made all the arrangements for me to go for summer tutoring so that I could be registered and be able to start the seventh grade in the Academia San Alfonso, under the administrative leadership of the Holy Cross nuns.

I was ready to start at my new Catholic parochial school when, suddenly, my parents moved back to the neighborhood. When Fela heard that they had come back, she decided to return me to my parents care arguing that "she (me) has become too arrogant and too much of herself." Fela had made the initial steps in enrolling me in the Catholic school, and with the return of my parents, I found myself alone and totally confused as far as what school I would go to. And Fela refused to help me in making the final school arrangements.

The following month was very stressful for me, a child of 11 years old. My parents were not interested in sending me to a Catholic school because there was tuition to pay, a uniform code, and a certain type of shoes to wear, and they did not have the money to pay for it. I would have been attending the school of the *riquitos* (rich people) of my hometown, and my parents were from one of the poorest areas of this town. They were not educationally sophisticated, and they could not make the distinction between public school and parochial school. They were not Catholic practitioners, either. I realized that I was on my own. I begged Fela again for help, but she again refused to help me.

That summer, I managed to register and attend the required four weeks of tutoring with *Señorita Josefina Pastrana*, a very unsympathetic unmarried retired teacher. I saw Miss Pastrana's eyes criticize me for what I did not know. The tutoring was conducted in the balcony of Miss Pastrana's house where all the people walking in the street heard her screaming and telling me how little I knew, and how sorry she was that I was attending this new school. She always compared me with the other four students who were part of the summer tutoring program. She said that I had "processing" problems, and she did not see me making it in that highly advanced academic school.

Although I was frustrated by the *innuendos*/negative comments of this teacher, I managed to complete the four-week program. I had won that small battle, then I needed to convince my father to allow me to go to this Catholic junior high school. And, after a week of lecturing my eighty-year-old father on the advantages of this school, and in order to get rid of my *ruegos* (begging), my father agreed to send me to this school and to buy all the necessary supplies, clothing, and shoes. Still today, I do not know where he found the money to pay for these things.

I registered in the Catholic parochial junior school myself. When the school officials gave me the tuition slip, I told the *Madre Superiora* (the principal) that my parents could not pay the tuition. I took my father to school and when the nun saw my octogenarian father, she agreed on charging me only $1 per month for tuition. "Another battle won," I thought.

I started school in mid-August. My teachers were two arrogant and disciplinarian American nuns, and a retired Puerto Rican teacher of Spanish. I also found that most of the classes were taught in English. In fact, I learned most of the school subjects (science, social studies, and mathematics) in English. And, although I was exposed to two languages simultaneously, I am sure that I missed a great deal of academic content because I did not understand what was being taught in English during those two years that I attended Academia San Alfonso. I just memorized the words and threw it back on tests. I remember listening to the book *Treasure Island,* which was written in English; then orally translated in Spanish, chapter by chapter, by the Holy Cross School nun. I never understood the cultural and psychological aspects in the novel. I was bored and very frustrated listening to the nun's translation. The nun told us what happens in each of the chapters, but we were not involved in the happenings of the story or in the richness of the language used. And, for two years (seventh and eighth grades) I struggled with the English language and with the nuns. One of the first things that I did was to understand the psychology of the nuns. I learned to smile at them, to accept what they said, and not to question them.

I also found that by thinking in Spanish and translating the lesson from Spanish into English, I was able to gain some understanding of what was going on in the classroom. One of the strategies that I employed was that once I was at home, I translated into Spanish the content given in school that day. I wrote and memorized long pieces of information, first in Spanish and then in English. I also reviewed mathematics and science problems and projects with my nephew, who was in a public high school but who was a very good student in mathematics and science.

My school peers accepted me immediately and identified me as a "smart girl." I did not think so, I just tried to find ways to understand the information covered by the teachers. But using all these strategies worked for me, I was able to pass all the requirements for the eighth grade. Miss Pastrana was wrong when she said that I was not going to be able to make it. I received the Social Studies medal, and, the Puerto Rican teacher told me that I was also supposed to get the Spanish medal too, but the nuns wanted to distribute the medals throughout all good students, not just necessarily the "best ones."

The Catholic school stopped at the 8th grade and if students wanted to continue in a Catholic high school, their parents would have to send them to the city of Caguas, about 45 minutes from Aguas Buenas by car. I realized that my parents could not afford the tuition and the transportation cost. I also realized that the only differences between the public and the parochial school were the climate and the academic status. All my peers from Academia San Alfonso went to Caguas, some to Notre Dame High School and some to the public high school. I went back to my town public high school. And to some extent, that was a blessing, because I started again to learn about the Spanish language and Spanish literature. I had the opportunity to learn about my Puerto Rican history and my own ancestral roots.

Life continued to be the same; the main highlights were attending school and visiting the plaza every Saturday night. I remember the crowded Saturdays; boys to one side, girls to the other, and so all the faces were looking at each other all the time. This happened every Saturday night, rain or shine. Every Saturday was a special night, in which the youngsters of the town went around and around the plaza while the married people sat in the benches with their small children, and observed the youngsters, while enjoying eating a *piragua, a dulce de coco or a pirulí.* The youngsters would not sit; they were in search of someone or using the time to be with someone. Usually, young men had already planned dates or had a particular girl in mind to search for. From these gatherings, many marriages were initiated or for others, it was the beginning of joining together as a couple.

One month later, after my eighth grade graduation, my parents moved again, this time closer to the town of Aguas Buenas. My father started to have disagreements with his older son (one of seven children from a previous marriage) and to avoid further misunderstandings, he decided to sell the small house and build another one in one of the poorest barrios of the town, on a *callejon*, a narrow dirt road. Although this house had two small bedrooms, the electricity never worked it, had an outside latrine, and we had to go outside to take a bath. But one of the advantages of this new location was that my mother started to work a couple of hours five days a week in a nearby house, selling and serving lunches to factory women. She was making a few dollars and she brought the leftovers food that became our dinner. My father continued to receive the $20 rent. My middle sister struggled with school, and a few months later she quit school and moved in with a middle class family taking care of their three children.

On the first day of high school in Aguas Buenas, I walked down a narrow, mountainous street toward the school. I did not like the physical appearance of the school, but I had no other choice but to stay there. The two years that I spent in the parochial school had changed my vision of what a school was, but I found the strength to forget my 'ideal school,' and I entered this one. I looked at my schedule, and one of the courses was Spanish Literature, to be taught by a Mr. Díaz.

"I hope I learn something in this class," I thought with little enthusiasm.

I went to the Spanish Literature class and sat in the middle of the classroom, and I was surprisingly impressed with the teacher, who was a bold small man. He smiled at the same time, but his voice evoked seriousness about what he was lecturing. He talked about the history of the Spanish language, its evolution and the anecdotes behind the different pieces of literature that we explored in class. I listened to him explain the difficulties of Miguel Saavedra in writing his *Quijote de la Mancha*, and how, to some extent, the *Antonio Quijano, el Quijote*, reflected biographical facts of the writer. I sat, my mouth and eyes wide open, listening to Mr. Díaz explain that all of us behave like "Sanchos" as well as "Quijotes." He told us that Dulcinea del Toboso represented our own illusions. What a pleasure it was to listen to this man! I immensely enjoyed the time that I spent in this class. With a smile, Mr. Díaz recited poems from Unamuno, Rubén Darío, Gabriela Mistral, José Gautier Benítez, and Julia de Burgos.

"I want to be like Mr. Díaz. I want to be able to talk about all these people and motivate others, too," I thought while I listened to him.

I completed one year in this school, where I learned a great deal from Mr. Díaz. His voice, gestures, and deep knowledge are still with me. I started in the same school the following year, but I found that Mr. Díaz was no longer going to be my Spanish teacher. I was no longer satisfied with the school, and I realized that I could not stay. The students were very quiet, too passive. The teachers, with the exception of Mr. Díaz, asked students to just copy and memorize facts. I decided to change schools. I was able to reach one of my parochial school classmates who was attending a public school in Caguas. She told me that she was happy with her school and her peers. I immediately made a plan to go and register at the Caguas high school.

"I will talk to my mother to tell her that I am transferring to a high school in the neighboring town of Caguas," I thought.

My mother, as always, did not argue with me.

"*Pues mija, haz lo que tú quieras*," (Do whatever you want to do) she said.

Alone, I took the bus from Aguas Buenas to Caguas, and I went to the high school. I went to the principal's office.

"It is too late to give you a full program. Why do you come so late?" the administrator in charge of incoming students asked me.

"Well, I could not come before," I told her.

"You will have to wait because there are no available seats right now," the administrator told me.

"Ok, I will wait."

After one week of waiting at the Gautier Benítez High School principal's office, I was finally given an academic program. During that week of waiting, I observed the teachers, the administrators, and the students. I knew that I was going to like the school and that I was going to have the opportunity to continue to study and venerate the Spanish language and Spanish literature.

In this new school, I found good teachers, although not as good as Mr. Díaz. Through these teachers' guidance, I was able to read the work of José Ortega y Gasset, Alejandro Tapia y Rivera, Salvador Brau, Enrique Laguerre, Manuel Alonso, Gabriela Mistral, Pedro Carpentier, Manuel Fernández Juncos, and Benito Pérez Galdós. The Spanish language and the history of Spain and Latin America helped me to learn more of my ancestry and my roots, and assisted in my affirmation of my Puerto Rican identity.

When I compared both schools (the one in Aguas Buenas and the one in Caguas), I found that the primary difference of the schools was not in the academic curriculum; it was in the climate of the school and in the type of students that attended the school. My Caguas classmates were more cosmopolitan, more outspoken, more self-motivated, and more determined than those in the Aguas Buenas high school. The complexity of the city, the variety of programs and courses offered, and the variety of teachers teaching the same subject area, contributed to students' empowerment. I am so glad that I went to this high school. I did well in this Caguas high school. I was able to participate in class discussions; teachers acknowledged my talents; and I was able to find two wonderful friends- Gladys and Mirta.

Gladys, Mirta, and I were inseparable until we graduated from high school, when each of us took different routes in life. Mirta was a bright high school student. She was very talented in science, especially biology, physics, and chemistry. Gladys was extremely talented in mathematics; algebra, geometry, and calculus. I was a good student of Spanish and English language and literature. We became a good trio. Gladys lived in a low-middle class neighborhood in Caguas; Mirta in a barrio of San Lorenzo, where her parents had a humble small food store. I lived in a poor barrio of Aguas Buenas. Although I visited Gladys and Mirta at their homes, I never invited them to my house; I was ashamed of my home conditions: house trapped on a *callejon*, with no electricity and an octogenarian father who was not friendly to visitors.

When several years later, I lost Gladys and Mirta, I felt that I had lost a wonderful network. Why did it happen? I really do not know. We became teachers in different towns, we engaged in graduate school in different schools and in different departments. We married, had children, and identified different priorities. Somehow, we substituted this network with something else. It was 40 years later that at a high school reunion, I saw Mirta again. Although we did not recognize each other, we did recognize our names. Mirta called Gladys and told her of our encounter, and we scheduled a meeting in my Isla Verde apartment. Gladys came in a wheel chair, affected by stomach bacteria that had immobilized her legs. A few months later, Mirta called me up in New York City to give me the sad news of Gladys's death. I thanked God for allowing me to see her again.

While in high school, I again changed my religious practices. I went from Catholic to Pentecostal. As long as I lived with Fela I went to the Catholic Church, and I was a Catholic practitioner. But once I graduated from the Catholic school, I was not as devoted as I was before. I continued 'being a Catholic,' although I no longer went to mass.

During this period when my faith was uncertain and unsettled , the Pentecostals arrived in my neighborhood in search of people to convert to Jesus Christ through their religion. They came to my house to try to convert my father and my mother, but my father always challenged them in their belief system. My mother, on the contrary, was indifferent to what Pentecostals said to her. As the last resource, they put their eyes on me. I found this group sincere and convincing, and I wanted to be a part of them. Since my parents did not care about my faith or religious practice, the Pentecostals had a free reign to adopt me into their faith. I started to visit the church, and a few months later, I was baptized as a member of the Pentecostal church.

My parents did not practice any religion, for them religion was not an important issue when raising my sisters or me. My father did, however, had an issue with letting me go with this group of people to night services, but I managed to convince him to allow me to go to some of them. For some reason, the Pentecostals did not work on trying to convert my sisters.

I quickly became very popular in the Pentecostal church. I memorized pages and pages of the Bible; I became a Sunday school teacher for the children, and a Sunday street preacher. The church leaders would send me with a small group of members to preach in the corners of the town of Aguas Buenas. I took a portable microphone and in a very loud voice I repeated the following phrase many, many times:

"Si no te conviertes a Cristo vas a ir al infierno. Tienes que venir a Cristo a través de la Iglesia Pentecostal." (If you do not convert to Jesus Christ, you will go to hell. You need to become a Pentecostal.)

The Pentecostal church officers loved my performance because 'the prodigious girl' attracted a lot of people who stopped to hear the Lord's message. I was the miracle girl: a Catholic adolescent, graduated from the prestigious Catholic school *Academia San Alfonso*, who had been converted to the Pentecostalism. I had no supervision, and I said whatever came to my mind. Fela and her husband, both Catholic practitioners, could not believe what they heard from other people who saw and heard me. One day while I was preaching, I saw Santos standing in a far corner with his head down listening to my preaching. My parents were totally indifferent; they never made a comment about these Sunday street performances.

One day, the Aguas Buenas mayor's office planned a Sunday trip to the beach of Luquillo (about a two- hour bus ride) on a Sunday. I had never seen or touched the sea! I was so excited about the idea of going swimming at the beach that I ran to city hall and signed my name without consulting or asking permission from the Pentecostal officers. My parents allowed me to go since there were other adults from the *barrio* who would be there, too.

The day of the trip, I was sitting in the bus contemplating the tall trees while the bus moved toward the coast of the island. I suddenly saw that green-blue body of water, and the more I went toward it, the smaller it became. When I arrived at

Luquillo Beach, I contemplated the immense sea. It was so beautiful! I instantly felt relaxed, and happy, and I went into the water. This was my first encounter with big spaces of water, the incredible salted water: the sea.

I went back to Aguas Buenas after seeing and tasting the sea. I was still very happy and very relaxed. And I thought that I still had time to go to the night Pentecostal service. I went home, and I asked my father permission to go to church. I changed clothes and headed to the night service. I was very dark, my skin looked blackish-red; my hair was kinky; and my eyes were red. But I was very happy! After sitting down in one of the seats of the church, I began to notice that my brothers and sisters were very serious with me, concentrating and not looking at me. They said things that I did not understand like: "You abandoned the church to go to the beach," "How could you do something like that?" "You left God for the sins of the beach," And, immediately, the officers received the Holy Spirit and bombarded me with:

"*Te vas a ir al infierno por estar compartiendo con impíos; abandonaste la casa de Dios*" (You will go to Hell, you abandoned the house of God,)

I was surprised, overwhelmed by the noise and the hysteria, and I wanted to stand up and run. However, *I* stayed until the end of the service. While all these individuals confronted and insulted me, I cried, not because I was ashamed of what I had done, but of what they were doing to me. They were abandoning me. At the end of the service, I stood up, and finally was able to get out of the church, and I had no intention of coming back. I ran and ran until I was in front of my house.

Two weeks later, the minister, his wife, the 'elders,' and the young members of the church, all came to my house several times to ask me to go back. But they never apologized for the insults. I never went back. My parents did not ask me what happened; it is like they were not interested in finding out. None of my family members questioned me on why I stopped going. However, the whole town commented on my strange escape from the Pentecostal church.

One year passed. I felt very lonely and in need of a religious affiliation. I then went to the Baptist Church as a refuge for my spiritual anxiety and relentlessness. This church opened its doors to me, although they always talked about my difficulties with the Pentecostal church. I, however, tried to forget the bad experience, and concentrated on studying very hard, and staying in school, trying to memorize all the information given to me by my teachers and books. However, I found that I had difficulties finding friends. I tried to reach my parochial school peers, but they were unreachable; they had their own friends and priorities. I was not able to find friends around my neighborhood. Mirta and Gladys lived far away. And, because I did not have friends, I could not enjoy the weekly Saturday night walks, although I had two or three dresses ready to go to the plaza.

Doña Benita, one of the town seamstresses did miracles with the cloth fabric that my mother bought from *El Arabe, the quincallero*. She made me three dresses, and they looked exactly like those modeled by the Anglo girls of the catalog. How we got those magazines in our homes is unclear to me, but by looking at those magazines, I decided on the type of dress I wanted to have. Once I made my mind in terms of what type of dress I wanted, I took the material that my mother bought from the *quincallero* and I went to Doña Benita, who, for 10 or 15 cents, replicated the dress for me. But, because I had no friends to go to with to the plaza, I did not wear them on Saturdays. I sometimes wore them to do errands for my mother or neighbors. I felt lonely, in spite of having so many people around me!

Loneliness did not stop me from reading and doing well in school. In the twelfth grade, I was selected the treasurer of the graduating class, and at the end of the year, I graduated with honors. My parents could not go to my graduation ceremony, because my father was too old and unable to walk. My mother could not free herself from the job that was bringing food to the entire family. I could not go to the graduation party, either, because it was during the night in the neighboring town of Caguas, and I did not have anyone to take me. Despite not celebrating, I received an invaluable gift: I was accepted at the University of Puerto Rico, and I was offered an academic scholarship. I wanted to be a lawyer. If not, I wanted to be a teacher, I wanted to teach the same way as Mr. Díaz, I thought.

An Activist Scholar

María Torres Guzmán

My life is clearly centered around the circular migration many Puerto Ricans experience. The questions I have asked myself are: what are the signs of this migration in my life? How does the experience of going back and forth make sense to me?

I was born in Puerto Rico but shortly after my mother, with me in her arms, and two older sisters flew to Detroit, Michigan to reunite the family. My father had migrated from Puerto Rico just a few months before my birth. The political winds in Puerto Rico had changed and my father feared the pro-statehood party would not create a favorable employment context for him. He decided to go north to join his brother-in-law, Tio Geraldo, in the steel industry. My father, mother and three children, all girls, lived on Bagley Street, in the already settled Mexican barrio, which had established around Most Holy Trinity Church, which had a traditionally Irish influence. The place we went to was multilingual and multicultural.

By the age of four, I wanted to go to school. Despite my father's attempts to get me enrolled, everywhere we went would come back with a "but she is too young, Mr. Torres." I entered kindergarten at Most Holy Trinity Parish School, the school my sisters attended. They were my language models as they were already learning English in school. My English environment schooling came to a halt when I was 12 years old. We returned with my mother to Puerto Rico.

In Puerto Rico, I was placed in an advanced class. My grades in elementary school were great and I was picking up Spanish quickly. I was like a sponge and my desire to do outstanding work in school, whether in English or in Spanish, never weaned. I took the SAT when I was in eleventh grade and graduated during the summer at Ponce High School when I was 16 years old. My path to the University of Puerto Rico in Rio Piedras was a given.

While my father was a laborer in the steel industry and my mother alternated between being a housewife and a seamstress, never was there doubt that we would attend college. My mother had attended primary school and my father had continued through business school after graduating from high school.

On my father's side one of my cousins became a teacher and so did my eldest sister, but I never thought about teaching as a career. I mused about becoming an industrial engineer, an architect, and a painter. I was great at math. Yet, I ended up in Spanish Language and Literature. Language had become central to my scholarship.

Our family was split again by the time I finished my undergraduate work. My parents were back in Michigan with my two younger brothers and the middle sister. The eldest sister was now married and in California. I remained in Puerto Rico. I had finished my undergraduate and was planning to go back for an MA, but during the summer I visited my family in Michigan and stayed. I received a scholarship to attend the University of Michigan in Ann Arbor and finished an MA in Romance Languages and Literature.

From Ann Arbor, I went to Detroit. My days of activism in the Detroit Latino Community drew me to the Chicano-Boricua Studies Program at Monteith College, a defunct general education college within Wayne State University. Language, culture, and ethnic identity were all intertwined in my life as a young faculty member where I taught many students who had been my classmates in elementary school, my sisters' best friends, and family members. I was much invested in making sure that these and all the rest of the students receive a fair chance as I had benefited from my time in Puerto Rico and I could see that there was something about knowing who you are that provides the strength to go beyond what you grew up with.

During the years at Wayne State, bilingual education came into existence and I began to see this innovative educational program as worthwhile pursuing intellectually. My immediate interest came from a project my students had engaged in where they documented what was going on in the bilingual programs in the city. I was a figure in the education world of the city and had, from a policy perspective in my education committee role in New Detroit, a coalition of leaders from civil rights and advocacy organizations, that there were tensions between the critical mass necessary for bilingual education to take place and the Bradley vs. Millikan desegregations case which would try to disband any critical mass of Latinos. I became a signatory to the case and argued for bilingual education as a potentially integrative structure that would be based on the students understanding who they were, enjoying the rich heritage and traditions. The understanding related to the complexity of social justice as different communities come together to solve historical discrimination became a motivating intellectual force in my life.

I went to Stanford University to find some answers. Little did I know that many more questions would emerge; some still remain. As an activist scholar, I focused on parental involvement in schools as participatory democracy for my dissertation topic. From then on, I would continue to pursue – through practice and research – answers to my many questions.

For a period of time, I worked at the Intercultural Development Research Association under Dr. Jose Cardenas. This work expanded my practice and understanding of education as I worked with school districts throughout the state and beyond. It also picked up the theme of desegregation and integration with respect to bilingual education. I still had some intellectual longings and decided to move into academia.

After a stint at Michigan State University, I moved to New York City. I started at Teachers College, Columbia University in 1986. I decided that I had to walk my talk with my own daughter and enrolled her in the first dual language education program in the city, PS84.

I started observing classrooms, working with teachers, and beginning what I believe has been my professional life's work – continuous dialogue with dual language teachers about their development, their wondering, and their concerns. As the programs expanded, I moved to work with a group of supervisors at the district level. I helped design the Dual Language Middle School and moved to work with PS165 when Ruth Swinney, the then district coordinator, became its principal. While I still continue in NY City, my return to Puerto Rico is continuous. I spent my first sabbatical year there and worked documenting work in San Juan Domingo School in Guaynabo. It was an experience of working with an underprivileged community in my homeland that gave renewed focus to my work – language and culture were only one set of issues; social class was also significant.

Confesión de Una Maestra

Con una cara bien triste
entró a mi oficina ayer,
preocupada una maestra
para hacerme una consulta.
Ya han pasado muchos años
en este ministerio santo
de muchas noches de vela
y largos días de búsqueda.

Por qué será que yo siento
que no cumplo mi misión,
que en esta dura tarea
a todos los que yo enseño,
nunca aprenden por igual.

Presa de entusiasmo y afán
desde ese saloncito alegre,
a muchos doy con amor
ese pan del intelecto
pero no todos los que yo enseño,
aprenden ya por igual.

Predico el don de la idea
y mucha práctica yo profeso.
Crean, buscan, recrean entendimiento,
pero a todos los que yo enseño,
nunca aprenden por igual.

Recomiendo el libro, de todos un gran amigo
que abre puertas hacia el conocimiento,
y da paz al espíritu revuelto,
pero a todos los que yo enseño,
nunca aprenden por igual.

Ya mi voz apenas si se nota
aunque ellos oyen y repiten con amor,
pronuncian, repiten y retienen.
Soy ejemplo de la fuerza del lenguaje,
lengua inmortal de antepasados nuestros.
La pronuncian, la leen y la escriben
pero a todos los que yo enseño,
nunca aprenden por igual.

Soy mensajera peremne de la enseñanza
motivación, esfuerzo y esperanza,
con un mensaje de expectaciones altas.
Y aun así, aquellos que yo enseño,
no todos aprenden por igual.

¡Quién en este momento de su vida
no recuerda a su maestra favorita!
La fuerte, la brillante, y sobre todo,
la que no duerme, planeando toda la noche,
pero a todos los que yo enseño.
nunca aprenden por igual.

La escuché con atención
fe, esperanza y ánimo yo le dí,
y con mucho respeto, señores
a esta maestra yo calmé.

Chapter 4

TURNING POINTS

There was the curved mountain road, leaving small cement and wooden houses behind, crossing trees and gardens in those cool mornings on the hill. There were the *campesinos* drinking their black coffee and looking out at the enormous town of Río Piedras and the San Juan bay in the horizon to the north. It took me two hours to get from Aguas Buenas to Río Piedras in a *público*, traveling through the curved road of the mountains, then to the *Carretera Militar*, and then to the city of Rio Piedras, a city buried on the premises of small and big shopping stores, its plaza surrounded by buses and *públicos* waiting to take people to the outskirts and to near and far *pueblos*.

The público left me in front of the plaza. I walked north for about 20 minutes to find the University of Puerto Rico (UPR) and the building where I had my first class, *El Colegio de Pedagogía*/The School of Education. I saw stores and large houses converted into *pensiones* (boarding houses). Then, there I was, in front of the famous *Torre de la Universidad de Puerto Rico*, a tower that symbolizes the power that this academic center has had on the preparation of young minds to become the leaders of Puerto Rico.

"This is an important day for me," I thought.

It was my first day at the University of Puerto Rico, Rio Piedras Campus, which was, many would argue, the best campus in the system. And I repeated again and again:

"Yes, I know that this is an important accomplishment. I need to do well and succeed." But, I was scared of this new world.

The University of Puerto Rico was established by an act of the insular Legislature in 1903 to "provide the inhabitants of Puerto Rico as soon as possible, with the means of acquiring thorough knowledge of the various branches of literature, science, and mechanical arts including agriculture, and mechanical trades, and with professional and technical courses in medicine, law, engineering, pharmacy, and in the science and art of teaching." The government of Puerto Rico made provisions for the attendance of deserving students to different educational institutions in Puerto Rico through the establishment of scholarships, thus making it possible for the bright students in the remote *barrios* within the island to be carried through to graduation at the best university. Because of this mandate of the Legislature at the beginning of the 20th century, seven decades later, I was able to come to UPR by receiving an academic scholarship.

Once I was accepted at UPR, I thought about a lot the professional careers that interested me: law, social work, communication, and, of course, teaching. But at the same time, I was looking for a quick teaching degree that would give me the credentials to get a full-time job. I remembered when I received the application papers to apply to college, I looked for the fastest program since I had no money, and I was eager to work as soon as possible. Also, my family was looking forward to me bringing some money home. The fastest degree was a two-year teaching certificate. I found my interest in teaching when in high school, one of my Spanish teachers let me conduct the class for a short period of time, and I had enjoyed the experience. I was able to introduce the writer Manuel Alonso and his poem *Poesía Puertorriqueña*, which was written in Old Spanish.

I enrolled in the *Programa Normal*, a two-year provisional teaching certificate program to teach in grades 1-6 elementary schools. The scholarship that I received covered my tuition and books and provided me with a small monthly stipend. This stipend was a blessing, because with it I could pay the *público* every day, afford a meal a day, and purchase some clothing and shoes.

How was my first day at UPR? I remember that I was proud and happy to be at the *Torre de la UPR*, looking for the *Colegio de Pedagogía*. I had never seen this tower before, although I had read about it and I had seen pictures of it. It was really impressive, especially the street where it was located. There was a small pedestrian path, joining the Tower with the famous Ponce de León Avenue. This small path had palmas reales (a special type of palm tree) on both sides of the street. It looked respectful, illustrious, and beautiful. After admiring the tower, I asked for the location of the *Colegio de Pedagogía*, and I headed toward it. I found my classroom, and I started my day with enthusiasm and dedication- forward to teaching.

My first year at the university was very stressful. I found myself in a strange academic environment taking very challenging courses. First, because I had performed well in the entrance examination, I was placed in an honors English class. I found that I was not ready for the class. Most of the students were fluent English speakers, and the professor conducted the class on the assumption that every student was at the same proficiency level. Although I did not fail the class, I did not do well. The following semester, I requested a change and I was placed in an intermediate English class where I understood the content and the tasks assigned by the professor. In addition, the UPR was piloting a new course in the area of mathematics. "Modern Mathematics" was taught for the first time, emphasizing math concepts beyond the operational aspects. I had a hard time following the logic of the course because the professor jumped from one topic to the other without fully explaining any of them. Both students and professor were lost. And the tests were given at night, the same test for the entire student population taking the course, around five to eight hundred students. I had to make arrangements to stay overnight in Rio Piedras in order to take these tests. The most difficult part was explaining to my old man father why I had to sleep outside the house. I also had difficulties with my philosophy teacher. I was not able to follow her discussions and I had difficulties connecting the readings and her lectures. There were, however two courses that I really enjoyed: Spanish Literature and Introduction to Teaching. Somehow, I was able to manage to pass all of these courses, and get a decent academic record to maintain my financial scholarship for the following year.

At the beginning of my second year at UPR, I met another student who was in the same *Programa Normal*, who, like me, was studying to become a teacher. We started dating and by the completion of the program we were engaged.

That same year my mother and my sisters and I were able to convince my father to move to the house that he owned and that was providing him with the $20 every month. I promised that as soon as I received a salary I was going to be in charge of the finances of the house. It was a very small old house, but it was in a better part of town and it had running water, electricity, and a bathroom. My mother, who paid into social security through her part-time job, was now in her sixties and was close to apply for social security benefits.

After completing my two years, I received the *Diploma Normal* and my teaching certificate. There was no graduation, no roasted pig, no *piña colada*, and no celebration. But I was ready to earn my first check. I sent out my teaching application, and I indicated that my own town of Aguas Buenas was my preferred place to work.

Usually, "normalistas" (two year college teachers) go to the most remote areas to teach for one or two years. These teachers left their homes very early in the morning, headed on Monday to the rural school and came back on Friday evening.

Mr. Ramirez, the school superintendent, interviewed me. And, when I said that I needed to work and I wanted to become a good teacher, he took that as meaning that I did not care where he was sending me, as long as he provided me with a job.

He sent me to the most remote rural school in town: Mulitas Alvelo. All year, he kept saying at general meetings:

"Miss Reyes wants to become an excellent teacher; she does not mind starting her teaching career in Mulitas Alvelo. I sent her to this school so that she can get teaching experience and become a good teacher."

I did go to Mulitas Alvelo. I stayed in Don Felipe's house the entire week, paying him a total of $20 a month for room and meals. The school was composed of three teachers who all stayed at Don Felipe's house. Fortunately, one of the teachers had bought a four by four Jeep truck, and every Monday, we endured the climbing of the difficult hills of the dirt road, which were worse when it was raining. I remember the many rainy, muddy, slippery mornings when Mr. Marcano, the owner of the Jeep truck, had to put all the *"refuerzos"* (strong engine gears) so that the engine could resist the incline of the hill. On many occasions, the Jeep stopped in the middle of the slippery dirt road, and Mr. Marcano would turn off the engine, wait a few minutes while Ms. Rosario (the other teacher) and I made the Sign of the Cross before he would attempt to start the truck again. At the end of the month, we contributed $20 dollars to Mr. Marcano for the four roundtrips to Mulitas Alvelo.

The school was within walking distance from Don Felipe's house. What an experience I had! I met great people, very poor ones, but with great hearts and who were very appreciative of their teachers. Mr. Ramirez was right- that was the right school for me to initiate my teaching career.

When I arrived at the Mulitas Alvelo Elementary School for the first time, I looked around and saw three simple classrooms made of wood with an uneven cement floor. There was simplicity in the rooms and in the students. The school was located at the top of a mountain, surrounded by many very dark green trees. Teaching was close to heaven, and I did not mind the physical conditions of the three available rooms. Three teachers were assigned to the school; one teacher was in charge of first and second grades, another teacher had third and fourth and I was in charge of fifth and sixth. We had one grade in the morning and another grade in the afternoon. I taught all the subject areas including English, Spanish Language Arts, Mathematics, Social Studies, and Science.

The English supervisor was Mrs. Monteverde, an old woman from the southern United Sates. At the beginning of the school year, Mrs. Monteverde decided to rent a horse to get to Mulitas Alvelo's school to observe the three teachers teaching English as a Second Language. I had heard many stories about how cruel she was to non-English- speaking teachers. She decided to observe me first. After observing me she was not satisfied with my English pronunciation in teaching language patterns using the *Fries English Series*. She interrupted me several times, and in front of the students, very slowly said the correct pronunciation. She told me that my pronunciation was really bad, and she spent the whole afternoon teaching me how to pronounce certain sounds in English such as *thumb, model, year, earth*. After that observation, I think she gave up on me, because she never went back to my classroom or communicated with my colleagues or me. Or, perhaps, she did not like the idea of getting to the school by horse. The year passed, and we never heard from Mrs. Monteverde again.

The students I taught at Mulitas Alvelo were almost adolescent (12 to 14 years old) and who came to the three-room elementary school with enthusiasm, faith, and a lot of hope in their teacher and on what the future would provide them. Most of these students came barefoot, hungry, and with very old and simple clothing. And, although the challenges of living in one of the poorest areas of the island forced them to be absent during the tobacco, coffee or orange seasons, once they came to school, they were attentive, motivated, and ready to learn. Every student was different, requiring special teaching techniques and motivational strategies. But what did I know at that time? I was a new teacher, recently graduated, with student teaching practice in one of the *urbanizaciones* (urban residential developments) of the San Juan metropolitan area, made up of middle class residents and students. Today, reflecting on what I did with those students, I don't think that I was prepared for the type of teaching those children needed. However, I tried to help them as best as I could. I did not have the knowledge, although I was interested in their learning and overall well-being, which was a good start.

Two of my students that year, Alejo and Arquimedes, were in sixth grade and still could not read simple sentences. They were the oldest students in their class, and their faces reflected the challenges of poverty, especially hunger, abandonment, and illiteracy. Their parents sent them to school when they were not needed in the field to pick the coffee beans or oranges or take care of the cows. I do not know how motivated they were to come to school but, the time spent in school was probably easier for them than working on the farms.

Alejo and Arquimides were not liked by the other students in the class because, in addition to being the oldest and the biggest of the class, they did not allow the other students in the class to do their work. They distracted them by talking or playing with them and they pushed them and took their personal belongings. What's more, Alejo and Arquimedes would hit those classmates who pointed to them and boldly said:

"Even though you're so big, you still do not know how to read or write."

In all sense of the term, they were "problem students," always fighting and bothering the other students. One day, I took them aside, and I had a conversation with them about their behavior:

"I am not happy with the way that you are acting in class, especially when you interrupt my lesson. I am also concerned because you do not participate in class. Hey, it is not too late to learn to read and write, and I am going to help you to learn."

Their smiles told me that they were ready for the challenge. Every day, while the rest of the students were reading their grade level basal reading, Alejo and

Arquimedes were beginning to identify the phonemic sounds and symbols of the Spanish alphabet:

carro- ka-rro;   tabaco- ta-ba-co;   vaca- va-ca-

They became interested in this learning activity and they came to school as frequently as they were allowed to. I tried to help them as much as I could, although I was inexperienced in the teaching of a complete developmental reading sequence. I did not know how to teach reading well, but I tried my best.

One day, a Thursday before *El Día del Maestro*, the Teacher's Day holiday, which in Puerto Rico is celebrated on the first Friday of May, one of the boys surprised me. In Puerto Rico, on Teacher's Day, teachers did not go to their individual schools, but they were invited to attend a Teacher's Day celebration, which was usually sponsored by the mayor of the town and the superintendent of schools. And, we, the three teachers of the Mulitas Alvelo School were leaving the school early that Thursday afternoon to attend the celebration. I noticed that Alejo did not show up to school that Thursday morning.

"Have you seen Alejo today? Does anyone happen to know if he is sick?" I asked.

I was concerned about this student, because for two months until this Thursday, he had come to school on a regular basis.

"No, Missi, we have not seen him," my students replied.

It was almost 11:00 AM (students were dismissed at 11:30 AM), and the class was getting ready to be dismissed. Suddenly, I saw Alejo standing in the door of the classroom. He stopped at the door and looked at me, and I noticed that he had a small bag in his hands. After a few seconds, he came to the front of the class and gave me the bag. I opened the bag, expecting to find a letter explaining his tardiness. And then I understood. I opened the bag to find three handkerchiefs and a plastic flower. Tears ran down my cheeks when I opened the gift, and I embraced him and thanked him. He had come to school late because he asked his mother to go to the nearest store to buy me, his teacher, a gift, to celebrate Teacher's Day. There were no stores in the barrio; the closest one was about ten miles from the school. After that, I understood how much he valued the little teaching that I was doing for him. Alejo, although he was not the greatest reader, began to learn that sounding letters and putting the sounds of the letters together was the first step in learning to read.

I stayed an entire year in that remote school and I will never forget the children, the parents, Don Felipe's family, or the community. Although it was a very challenging experience, I did enjoy my stay and my teaching at Mulitas Alvelo. Those students reflected poverty and educational neglect; however, they also reflected a tremendous desire to learn. They were motivated to walk three or four miles every day on dirt roads or narrow paths to come to school, in spite of all the challenges they confronted. There were days that they could not come, due to rain, to illness or because they had responsibilities on their parents' small farms. Because of the lack of resources at home- no electricity, no notebooks, no regular meals, they did not learn as quickly as perhaps they could have. They were absent often, but they always demonstrated an appreciation for the work of their teacher. On Fridays, even when they did not have much food in their own homes, they brought me bananas, plantains, eggs, chicken, or pork in appreciation of the week of teaching I had given them.

Due to the remoteness of the location, I asked the superintendent, Mr. Ramirez, to transfer me to a closer school the following year. Mr. Ramirez sent me to another rural elementary school, closer to the town of Aguas Buenas. I spent one year in that school. This school was departmentalized and I was able to teach social studies and Spanish to fourth, fifth and sixth grade students, though I was challenged to find instructional materials to teach these subjects. I used to spend long nights looking through books and trying to adapt those materials to my students' levels and ages. I remember getting to the school one hour before the starting time to copy on the board pieces of the materials I had found the night before.

I had almost completed my second year of teaching when my 93 year old father became very ill. His heart became weaker and weaker. He was hospitalized, and he never came out. One night, it was about 11 PM; I heard a strong knock on one of the front windows of our little house. I opened the window, I looked around, and I did not see anyone. I closed the window, and I went to sleep again. One hour later, a police officer came to the house to inform us that they had received notification by telegram that my father had died. I was overwhelmed with sadness and sorrow. I thought of the many hours I spent talking to him about his favorite piece- eternity, the existence of God, the mysteries of the Roman Catholic Church, and death. Although at times it was difficult to be raised by an old man, he was still my father, I loved him very much. I was heartbroken when he died.

Six months after my father's passing my fiancé and I married. We established our residence in the city of Caguas and embarked on a life of struggles and challenges. Two years later, my widowed mother moved in with me.

While I was teaching, I continued to attend UPR on Saturdays to finish my baccalaureate degree. After completing my baccalaureate degree, I was able to work as a Spanish teacher in a junior high school in the nearby city of Caguas. I was appointed to teach ninth grade Spanish class in Caguas. This too was a challenging school; the students were adolescents who came mainly from public housing and single families. They did not want to come to the classrooms, and once inside, they talked all the time, fought each other, and refused to do any academic work. I had five groups of students daily with 50 or 60 students in each group. Every night, I struggled to find strategies to motivate these large groups of adolescents. I used songs, poetry, dialogues, and controversial newspaper articles to motivate them to read and attempt the literacy tasks. Dramatizations were part of my daily lessons. Every Friday, I selected the best 10 students of the week, those that tried the hardest, and I awarded them with a copy of a written popular song signed by me. Since they had heard the song, they also wanted to have it written. It worked! These students read and worked very hard to get one of those songs. At the end of the day, I was exhausted and my feet hurt but I was satisfied with the academic progress of my students. One of those students was Antonio.

Antonio was a ninth grade student and a student leader, the president of the graduating class, though he was arrogant and constantly tried to be in control of his classmates. Throughout the year, I had tried to change Antonio's negative behavior because I recognized that inside him, there was a very intelligent human being, and I knew he could go far with his intelligence and his leadership abilities. After class, I would stay with him, coaching him and pushing him to change his behavior. I did not succeed, although I even confronted him in class. He always left me with an ambiguous smile that I was never able to read.

One day, at the end of the academic year, I entered the classroom and found Antonio very agitated and confronting his classmates. I was not surprised because Antonio was talkative, impulsive, and sometimes a little 'fresh' in class. I asked the class:

"What is the problem? What is going on?"

No one answered me. I went on with the class, and the days passed until it was the day of the graduation ceremony. At the ceremony, Antonio stood up and in front of the entire audience (composed of graduating students, parents, and guests) asked me to stand next to him:

"Miss Reyes, do you remember that day when you entered the class and all of my classmates were arguing with me? My classmates fought with me because I bought something for you without consulting with them. They do not understand that when I saw this ceramic flamenco doll (he pulled a doll out from a wrapping paper), it reminded me of the many days you tried to teach me Spanish, and most importantly, those times that you tried to change my impulsive character.

"When I saw this doll, I knew that I had to buy it, even though my classmates wanted to give you something else," Antonio continued. "But you know what I did? I paid for the doll with my own money. Because you did not get tired of me. You were persistent, and in spite of my bad behavior, you respected and helped me. This Spanish doll represents my love for you."

What a tremendous message my student gave me: to never give up, to respect, and to help all students! Still today, after more than 40 years, I still have this Spanish flamenco doll.

During the years to come, my husband and I were blessed by two sons and one girl. My mother, had moved in with us by then, and she was a big help during those early years with my children. My mother-in-law and father in law, who lived nearby were also available in case my mother needed help. I was blessed by having these three grandparents near, to take care of our children when we were working or studying.

I continued taking courses toward my baccalaureate degree at UPR, taking two to three courses per semester on Saturdays. Once I finished with the baccalaureate degree, I continued spending all Saturdays at UPR until I received my master's degree in education, with a concentration in the teaching of Spanish at the secondary level and a minor in school supervision and administration.

Through my graduate studies, I had the opportunity to meet great professors who, at the same time, were accomplished writers. Among these were Enrique Laguerrre, Jorge Luis Porras Cruz, Concha Melendez, and Carmen Gómez Tejera, who left deep footprints in my knowledge base and in my beliefs. Laguerre's theory about the integration of the language and culture of the Mexican peninsula and the Caribbean Sea fascinated me. In his courses, I read the work of many Latin American authors who enriched my vision of the world and mankind. I was terrified of confronting Professor Porras Cruz (he had the reputation of being mean and never giving good grades), but once I met him, I found that he was extremely human. He also contributed to my understanding and appreciation for Hispanic ancestry and Spanish literature. He reminded me of the teacher I had always idolized, Mr. Díaz: knowledgeable, passionate, and human. Carmen Gómez Tejera gave me perspective from the secondary classroom. I remember her guidance in helping me to develop lessons that not only presented Spanish language and literature concepts, but that contributed to students' development of positive values and attitudes. Watching and interacting with all these professors motivated me to one day becoming a college professor. I dreamed on the idea of teaching adults at the college level.

It was while working towards my master's degree that I met Felicita (Fela), who is still today a good friend of mine. One semester, I registered for a course called *Puerto Rican Literature*, with the renowned Puerto Rican writer Enrique Laguerre. Fela, was also taking Laguerre's course. She, too, has a passion for Spanish language and literature, and we began to study together. Our love for Spanish literature took to the level of discussing pieces of writing beyond those assigned by Professor Laguerre. Fela is a powerful writer and orator; she writes prose that sounds like poetry, and she is also a powerful speaker and reciter. Fela worked 30 years in New York City as an educational staff developer. Still today, we count on each other for advice and guidance when preparing a document written in Spanish. She lives 2,000 miles from me, however, when I need someone to hear me and give me comfort, I pick up the phone and I call her. Her favorite phrase is:

"*No me digas*." (Don't tell me that.)

She listens to me and provides me with the mental energy to fight whatever battle I am facing. And we continue to share our love for the Spanish language and literature.

I finished my master's degree at UPR and continued with the rewards and struggles of raising a family and being a teacher. I consistently spent late nights preparing lessons and finding ways to motivate my students to do well in school and in society. I used every available piece of written material (i.e.; comic strips, newspapers, advertisements, commercial flyers) as motivational devices.

My husband was appointed as a principal of a small urban school, and he was satisfied and very much involved with his job. My two sons started school. Olveen, attended nursery school at Los Hermanos Portal, a very good nursery school in Caguas where he expanded his language, social, and communication skills. This early training prepared him for kindergarten. Barney also attended primary school and began to learn to read in Spanish. They attended pre-kindergarten and kindergarten at their father's elementary school. Angeles Ivette was a two-year-old toddler, and spent the day in the care of my mother and mother-in law.

A Teacher and a Writer

Judith Ortiz Cofer

Born in Puerto Rico and raised in Paterson, New Jersey, Judith Ortiz Cofer now makes her home in Georgia. She is a poet, essayist, and novelist, whose work explores the experience of being Puerto Rican and living, writing, and teaching in the United States. She is the author of eleven books in various genres.

Cofer's first novel, *The Line of the Sun* (1989), was named a New York Public Library Outstanding Book of the Year. The novel traces the experiences of a family that immigrates from a Puerto Rican village to a barrio in Paterson, New Jersey. Writing in the *New York Times*, Roberto Marquez praised the book for the "vigorous elegance" of its language, and called Cofer a "prose writer of evocatively lyrical authority, a novelist of historical compass and sensitivity." Her second novel, *The Meaning of Consuelo* (2003), tells the coming-of-age story of a Puerto Rican girl living in the suburbs of San Juan in the 1950s. A bookish adolescent, Consuelo must face the challenges posed by her parents' crumbling marriage and her younger sister's descent into mental illness. In a starred review, *Booklist* said, "Cofer combines the timeless clarity and moral imperative of folktales with the timely wit of keen social criticism in an absorbing portrait of a smart and compassionate young woman…" The novel received the Americas' Prize in 2003. She is also the author of *Woman in Front of the Sun: On Becoming a Writer* (2000), an autobiographical collection of essays, interwoven with poetry and folklore, and accounts of her life as a teacher and writer.

Her most recent young adult book (Call Me María, 2006) is a novel told in poems, letters, and prose, about the Puerto Rican-American immigrant experience. Maria's father has taken her to live in a cramped basement apartment in New York, while her mother remains behind in Puerto Rico. *School Library Journal* said, "Understated but with a brilliant combination of all the right words to convey events, Cofer aptly relates the complexities of Maria's two homes, her parents' lives, and the difficulty of her choice between them." Other books include the essay collection, Silent Dancing (1990), a New York Public Library Outstanding Book of the Year and winner of the PEN/Martha Albrand Special Citation in nonfiction; the prose and poetry collection, *The Latin Deli* (1993), winner of the Ainsfield Wolf Award in Race Relations, also selected for the 2005 Georgia Top

25 Reading List, a project of the Georgia Center for the Book; the short story collection, *An Island Like You: Stories of the Barrio* (1995), winner of the American Library Association's first Pura Belpré Prize in Young Adult Literature, and a Best Book of the Year of the American Library Association, and three collections of poetry: *A Love Story Beginning in Spanish* (2005), *Reaching for the Mainland (1987)*, and *Terms of Survival* (1987).

Judith Ortiz Cofer is the Regents' and Franklin Professor of English and Creative Writing at the University of Georgia.

The City

Powerful traveling bird, I share a dream with you.
Would you allow me to borrow your wings?
I want to go around Manhattan
all Manhattan in one hour.

Powerful traveling bird,
your weightless feathered wings
will take me in my dreams
in one of those endless nights.

Your wings will take me around
to the city of parades, musicals, and winter glow
glorious churches of all traditions and beliefs
shining towers, wide avenues, and crowded streets
I will see the struggles, the hopes
all coming together with respect and admiration,
dissenting , engaging, throbbing faces
beholding the city, with a powerful string.

Chapter 5

A Risky Decision!

After being a Spanish junior high school teacher for two years, I was hired as a high school Spanish teacher at José Gautier Benítez High School, my alma mater. These were the most rewarding years of my teaching career in Puerto Rico. I had the opportunity to teach Spanish language arts and Spanish literature. My students came from Caguas or the nearby towns and were motivated to learn. Although there were not enough textbooks for all students, I put students in pairs during reading or written projects. My students wrote essays on current literary issues, and they wrote poetry that was praised by their peers, parents, and teachers. I remembered Mr. Díaz and I tried very hard to emulate him.

Two years later, I received an invitation to teach in a private university as a professor of Spanish. I was honored to receive such invitation.

" I am happy to become a professor of Spanish," I said to my high school colleagues. "I will guide my students to become experts in Latin American and Hispanic literature. And, I am sure that some of my students will become writers like José Emilio González, Enrique Laguerre, and Trina Padilla."

I saw myself changing the lives of many of my future students. I saw them loving the Spanish language, venerating Puerto Rican heritage, truly understanding the work and message of many powerful writers. Moreover, I was making myself responsible for that achievement.

"We are glad to see you moving ahead. You love to teach," my Gautier Benítez colleagues said to me at a farewell lunch.

In May, with kisses and tears, I said good-bye to my high school students, and colleagues, some of them my former teachers. At home, everyone in the family was happy for this accomplishment. I was the first one in the family to become a college professor. I received many congratulatory messages. My mother and my mother-in-law emphasized their continued support and help with the three children. My husband was proud to have a wife in the professorship field.

In the town of the valley of Caguas, the town where Indian caciques fought to death for freedom and independence, the land of *El Josco* (A bull that is the main character in a short story written by Abelardo Díaz Alfaro), and the city of the famous poet José Gautier Benítez, I began my professorship journey. The mail came with an envelope from the college: it was my teaching contract.

"I am now in the professorship field. I was born to be a professor. No one or nothing would stop me," I willed myself to hope.

Two days later, I carefully read my teaching contract, and it stated "instructor," not "professor." Why not? Up to that day, everyone called me *maestra* (teacher), a sign of respect and recognition of the teaching profession. However, this contract just called me *instructor*. Why instructor and not professor? What are the differences between these two words? I kept asking myself these questions while reading and re-reading the contract.

"I need to ask someone at the college to explain these two terms for me," I thought."

I called the college's academic office, and I asked to speak with an available professor. I had explained that I had been hired at that college, and I wanted to ask an experienced professor some questions.

"I am professor Vázquez, how can I help you?" the professor asked.

"Oh, *gracias*. Would you be able to explain to me the difference between being 'a professor' and being 'an instructor'?"

"Sure," professor Vázquez said. "Instructor is an academic rank for individuals without a terminal degree, usually, those without a doctorate in their field."

"How does rank affect the salary and benefits of instructors?" I asked.

"Well, usually, salary and benefits are less," he said. "Because there are not many office spaces at the college, instructors may share offices with other instructors.

On the other hand, professors must have an office to be able to continue their research and academic work."

"How are instructors included in the daily academic life of the college?" I asked.

"Oh, yes. They are part of the daily life of the college; they can be members of committees, however they cannot be chairs of those committees. They cannot be department chairs, either," he answered.

"Thank you for the information. I will see you at the general faculty meeting next week," I said.

My first day came. It was my first day as an instructor, not as a professor. I attended an orientation meeting with about 150 people from academia: administrators, professors, and instructors. But no one was really talking to me. Professors were involved in sharing "current academic university issues" of the college. I sat, I took notes, and I looked around.

"What a fascinating and distinguished group!" I thought.

At lunch, I was assigned to a table of mostly experienced professors and instructors. I introduced myself and I tried to engage in an academic conversation but no one was interested in knowing who I was, and what I was going to teach. The group of individuals were involved in a heavy debate about how little their students knew and how pressured they were by the students themselves and by the administration to give satisfactory, or even good grades. And, I thought,

"Why are students not achieving the goals of these professors and instructors?"

In the afternoon of the same day, I received my teaching schedule. I was an instructor of basic Spanish language courses, with emphasis on teaching grammar and the structure of the Spanish language. My schedule was one in which I was on campus five days a week, Monday through Friday, teaching a load of five courses from early in the mornings until early in the evenings. For example, on Monday, Wednesday and Friday, I had a class at 8:00 AM, another class at 1:00 PM and another one at 4:00 PM, leaving the college campus by 6 PM. On Tuesday and Thursday, I had a class at 8 AM and another one at 3 PM. I immediately started to plan my teaching day in order to make sure that I was prepared for my students and that I had the necessary materials to distribute to them. I was extremely motivated, and I could not wait to start. Although I was not happy about not having my own place to work (instructors shared a round table in the library) and prepare for my classes, I looked forward to meeting my students and engaging with them in interesting linguistic issues and projects.

One year passed in which I only taught introductory Spanish language courses. I liked my students, although teaching them proved challenging due to their lack of many basic language and literacy skills. But these students constantly expressed their desire and willingness to learn. Each class consisted of 30 to 40 students, and in one hour, I did my best to meet all of their language and reading needs. I used literature to prompt them every day to go beyond the proper identification of a noun, an adverb, or the past participle of a verb, and into a world of meaning and beauty.

"In this stanza of the poem, *Puerto Rico*, written by José Gautier Benítez, what is the message the author is trying to convey to us?" I asked them.

¡Borínquen!, nombre al pensamiento grato

como el recuerdo de un amor profundo

bello jardín, de América el ornato

siendo el jardín América del mundo.

"I think that the author is trying to show his love for Puerto Rico." "It's like loving a human being." "He sees Puerto Rico as one of the most beautiful places in America," were students' responses.

Although I enjoyed these basic introductory Spanish language classes, I wanted to experiment with other more advanced courses. Since the first semester, I had asked the director of the department to allow me to teach one of the following courses: "Puerto Rican Literature," "The Romanticism," "El Quijote," or "The Latin American Novel." I had dreamed of teaching these courses since I had taught some of them at the high school level, and I had enjoyed them so much. There were so many projects that my students could do! I smiled when thinking about the conversations I had with my high school students when studying "El Quijote." I realized that I did not have a terminal degree, as in a doctorate, like some of the professors; however, I wanted to share what I knew with my students.

"When can I teach one of the advanced courses?" I kept asking my department chair.

"Well, those courses are left for senior faculty; they are more specialized and need experienced faculty," the division chair responded. "We have a group of professors who have returned from Spain or from the United States, and they want to teach those courses. Professor Martínez and Dr. Smith, for example, they are the ones who are regularly assigned to teach them."

It was the second semester of my second year at the college, and my teaching schedule was the same: five sessions of introductory Spanish.

In one of the regular monthly faculty meetings, the president of the college announced:

"My dear faculty: In order to keep teaching here, everyone has to get a terminal degree which for many of you means a doctorate. If you do not have a doctorate, I strongly recommend that everyone here finds ways to enroll in a doctoral program.

Accreditation of the university depends on the number of "qualified faculty," such as Professor Martínez and Dr. Smith."

And the president of the college continued:

"Additionally, instructors cannot be considered part of the group of "prepared and qualified faculty." In order to keep this job, instructors need to at least enroll in a doctoral program."

And, every month the president of the college said exactly the same thing. I was beginning to get tired of this monthly monologue.

"Can I get a doctorate?" I asked myself. "How?" "I have three children and there are no doctoral programs in education on the island. But, what is my future here in this college without a doctoral degree?"

I kept thinking about this issue, and the more I thought about it, the more convinced I became of the need to start working on getting a doctoral degree.

It was the beginning of September and I was sitting in the balcony of my house located in the *Valle del Turabo,* in Caguas. On the lower ground, the hilltops seemed unreachable from the outskirts. I thought again about getting a doctoral degree. I wanted to pursue advanced studies in the area of language teaching but not necessarily in Spanish alone. I felt pretty well prepared in the area of Spanish, and, remembering the president's words, she did not say that it had to be in the current area of teaching.

I recalled that someone once told me that doctoral programs were offered in the United States. So, I made the determination to get the catalogues of several universities in the United States. I also remembered that during the summer, I had taken an advanced Spanish methodology course with a professor who was a full-time professor in a university in New York City, and who came to Puerto Rico to teach at the *Universidad del Sagrado Corazon.* His name was Santiago Luppoli. I had enjoyed his class very much. He had given me his home address and telephone number. So, I called Professor Luppoli:

"Professor Luppoli: This is your former student, Angela Carrasquillo, from Puerto Rico. I am thinking about pursuing a doctorate, and I want your opinion. Do you think that I will be able to do it?" I asked him.

Professor Luppoli encouraged me to pursue the degree.

"But I cannot guarantee you that the university in which I work will accept you," he said. "Please apply to this university but also get several catalogues from other universities and apply to them."

I followed his recommendation. I sent for various catalogs and examined five doctoral programs. Because each application required an application fee, I only completed two applications for doctoral programs in United States. One of them was in the university where Santiago Luppoli was a professor. The second one was in Pennsylvania. I completed the application packet, including three references, the Graduate Record Examination/GRE scores, and the application fee. I put both applications in the mail.

My life as an instructor continued as usual; motivating students, getting by with poor facilities, and having a great desire to become a "real professor." Two months later, in the beginning of October, I received two letters in the mail. One was from Pennsylvania and the other one was from New York City. I was reluctant to open the letters for fear of being rejected.

"Sooner or later I need to know," I said. "If I am rejected, I will start looking for other places."

I opened the letters, and I was surprised that I had been accepted into both programs. One of them was in Bethlehem, Pennsylvania and the other one was in New York City.

I did not think it over; I decided to go to New York City, but I did not share my decision with anyone at home for fear of being discouraged. I had never seen the city, and I had heard that it was big and hard to live in. But I had also known that it was the home of many Puerto Ricans. What more, I had met Professor Luppoli, and I liked his teaching style.

"Dr. Luppoli, I am going to enroll in the university in which you presently teach," I told him over the phone.

"¡*Bienvenida*! Welcome!" he said. "You have my full support."

From the college where I was teaching, I called the Admissions office and by mail, I enrolled in a doctoral program where I could take courses in Spanish language and literature and allow myself to add elective courses in another subject area. I called Professor Luppoli and asked him to be my adviser, and he happily agreed. I mentioned to him that I wanted to specialize in Spanish education and English as a Second Language. He was not sure if that was possible, but he was eager to find out the possibility of such a combination of specializations. What a wise decision! Those English as a Second Language elective courses opened many doors of opportunity for me in the United States.

It was early November and I hadn't left for New York City, but I started to become a little nostalgic about my surroundings. I noticed that the city of Caguas, where my house and the college were located, was becoming a big commercial center, a big city with a little of the charm of the old Spanish-colonial town. It retained its spectacular view of the mountains, especially the Cordillera Central, that were surrounded by growing urban residential developments, the *urbanizaciones*, and sugar cane and banana farmlands. I knew that I was going to miss the beauty of the island, but I also realized that it was time for me to move on. I had made the decision to go to New York City, and it was time to inform my family at home. It was Friday evening, and when I arrived at home, there were relatives visiting us.

"I am going to New York City. I am going to study there to pursue a doctorate," I told them.

There was silence; none of the relatives said anything. Everyone looked at each other. Everyone was probably thinking that I was crazy, that I had lost my mind and my maternal instincts. My brother-in-law said:

"Mejor comemos tierra antes de hacer una cosa así." (We rather eat soil than make a decision like that)

My widowed mother, who was living with me at the time, looked at me and with a dropped jaw said:

"¿Tú no estás hablando en serio?" (You are not seriously talking about that?)

She left the room.

"Yes, I am," I said.

My mother-in-law never mentioned the topic to me. My husband was in a state of shock with my decision, and did not immediately react. Later on, he told me to go ahead and that he, with my mother, would take care of the house and the children during the first four or five months of my first college semester in New York City.

Once I had 'the approval' of my husband to move to the mainland United States, I immediately began to make arrangements. I knew that I would have to sell my Ford Pinto car because I needed the money to pay for my university tuition and for room and board for at least one semester.

By mid November, I informed the department chair of my decision to leave the college to pursue a doctorate. He only asked:

"When?"

"This coming February," I answered.

At the age of 30, with three children and no money, I made the biggest decision of my life: to move to New York City.

Two months later, February 4, my family brought me to the airport where I took an Eastern Airlines plane routed to the mainland United States.

One of my first struggles was to survive in a new city and foreign culture, with a second language and an unfamiliar academic world. I had never visited New York City before. I did not know anyone in New York City, which is an unbelievable fact, because Puerto Ricans always know someone in New York City. For this reason, I first flew from Puerto Rico to Philadelphia, where my husband had family, and then came to New York City by car. Tía Edna and Tío Chago volunteered to drive me to New York City, specifically to the university dormitory. I had already arranged housing and registration by mail, and everything was in order once I arrived in New York City.

It was early morning on February 5, and I found myself on a long wide road with many car lanes and with many unclear messages.

"This is the New Jersey Turnpike, the US 95; it goes from Maine to Miami," Tía Edna said.

I looked at a map I had bought in Puerto Rico before taking the plane. I traced the red map line of US 95.

"How could a road be so long and so wide?" I asked myself.

Tío Chago drove for two hours in which cars and very big trucks were our driving companions. Tío Chago decided to follow the route that he was familiar with, the route he took when visiting friends and family in the South Bronx. And, after two hours, New York City appeared slowly with the bleak coal-tinged skies of the New Jersey flatlands. Then, the city seemed to rise out of nowhere all at once, filling the sky. Its buildings looked like tombstones.

Half an hour later, we were in front of the famous George Washington Bridge, looking like a prince, surrounded by many servants- cars of different brands, colors, and prices. From the George Washington Bridge, Tío Chago turned south, crossed the south Bronx, and crossed over a small bridge, and suddenly, we were in Manhattan. He decided to take a large avenue all the way toward the south of the city. Later, I found that this was the famous Fifth Avenue.

We were looking for the Hudson Hall building, the place that was going to be my residence for the whole semester. We passed streets, very tall buildings, and, asking people here and there, we finally arrived at the university area. We asked where the Hudson Hall building was, the residence for graduate students. In fast English, we were routed toward Washington Square Park.

"Look at that building- it says library, which means that we are not too far," Tía Edna said.

A few minutes later, we were in front of Hudson Hall. I could not believe that this unpainted old building was the residence for graduate students. It was un-kept and old and not too far from the famous beautiful glassed library. Today, I accept the idea that graduate programs are costly to run, and that usually, the services provided to graduate students are the poorest ones. I went into the building and identified myself to the attendant.

"Oh, you are finally here! We began to be concerned about you, since classes started today," said the building student attendant.

"Yes, I know. My first class is today," I said.

The air was cold, and the welcome was cold, too. Tío Chago and Tía Edna said goodbye and headed back to Philadelphia. I took the old slow elevator up to my room. I could not believe the limited space of the room.

"Is this the space that I have to share with another graduate student?" I asked myself.

It was small, and contained two twin beds, two small desks, and a tiny closet. That was it! There was no kitchen and no bathroom. The co-ed, common bathroom was at the end of the hall. Nothing else!

This was my first encounter with New York City living; a small space with limited facilities.

Years later, I realized that limited space is a common phenomenon in Manhattan.

Have you been to New York City, specifically in Manhattan, and visited a friend who has lived in the same apartment for many years? It is not uncommon to find a bathtub- not a shower- in the middle of the kitchen. And, everyone who is living in the apartment needs to wait for everyone to leave the apartment or to go to their individual rooms (if they have one), in order to take a bath sitting in the kitchen bathtub. This is even more difficult when there are several people, especially children living in an apartment with, often, only one bedroom. Over time, I have seen several living spaces in New York City that leave a lot to be desired. In Puerto Rico, all houses, even the poor ones, have a separate bathroom. And usually, there is more than one bedroom.

I looked around at the small shared room. That was all that I had. And I said to myself:

"This is what I have, and somehow, I have to survive this reality. I need to find people that I can connect with them. I am in New York City and I cannot go back! Absolutely not!"

I sat on my tiny bed, with no bedspread, only a wrinkled sheet, and I began to think about those generations of Puerto Ricans who had come before me.

Although Puerto Ricans have migrated to New York City since Puerto Rico became part of the United States, the largest wave of immigration came between 1940 and 1960. During this period, politicians in Puerto Rico solved the human surplus by facilitating- sometimes forcing-the migration of Puerto Ricans outside the island, mainly to the United States. The Commonwealth government claimed that:

"Puerto Ricans coming to the mainland will not have major difficulties because Puerto Ricans are United States citizens, and as citizens, they are familiar with United States schooling; and they will easily take full advantage of opportunities, and will easily integrate and prosper. They will realize their American Dream."

No one mentioned that the English language barrier, poor housing facilities, and discrimination, had not allowed that American dream to come true for many of the Puerto Ricans living in the mainland United States. I remember reading in several books that discrimination was the biggest challenge for Puerto Ricans arriving in the mainland United States, especially to their first destination –New York City.

Puerto Ricans who left the Island for the mainland United States were mainly the *Afro-mestizo*, the working class, and the poor. Most Puerto Ricans came to New York City to ensure prosperity, that is, to be able to send money to those that stayed on the island. Those Puerto Ricans who left the island exchanged their island life of simplicity and contentment for a chance to improve their and their family's financial conditions. The 'American Dream' surely motivated Puerto Ricans to leave the island for a better life, especially the assurance of finding a job. But once they came to New York City, they were discriminated against due to their skin color, lack of education, poor job or professional skills, and lack of knowledge of the English language. To most Puerto Ricans, success did not happen, due to racial and ethnic prejudice and discrimination. However, the Puerto Rican government continued to facilitate migration to the United States mainland to supply the workforce with cheap labor for jobs in exchange for financial support and incentives for a Puerto Rican economy that was supposed to bring prosperity to the people who managed to stay on the Island. In other words, less poor people on the island meant more resources for the rich.

My first days at Hudson Hall passed very slowly; I felt insecure, lonely, and unhappy. I missed my three children, my husband, my mother, my friends, my house, my bed and unexpectedly, my bathroom and my Puerto Rico. I found myself walking the cold and windy streets of Manhattan more than I had walked in my entire life. And during those *caminatas sin destino*, (walking without a destination) I discovered *la Calle 14*, Fourteenth Street. This is a commercial avenue whose shops at the time, sold everything that Puerto Ricans and other Latinos needed to buy: cheap furniture, shoes, used clothing, and home tools. I was fascinated by the amount of people walking around and going into the stores. I just walked back and forth in order to kill time. I had no one to talk to. I had no relatives, no friends, and no peers. I had no money to even buy a good winter coat; the one that I was wearing was a spring coat given to me by one of my colleagues who had it in her closet in Puerto Rico for several years. The coats were expensive, and I could not spend the few dollars I had brought from Puerto Rico, for they needed to last for the four months of the semester. I went inside Mays Department Store (not to be confused with Macys), to look around, window shop, and think about all the things I would buy if I had had the money. How many times a day did I walk Fourteenth Street? I went west and east, then east to west. I felt so alone in a city with some many people!

Even since 1790, New York City has been identified as a populated city and it has been steadily populated since the 1940's, due to waves of immigration. Puerto Ricans came in big groups in the 1940s, 50s, and 60s. After the 70s, the number of

Puerto Ricans moving to New York City declined; it has been fewer and fewer since the late sixties although they continue to come. Today, although there are more Puerto Ricans leaving New York City than those arriving, the birthrates of those who stay maintain the high number of Puerto Ricans in New York City.

The Puerto Rican population in New York City has been growing, not shrinking as many people would think. What really happens is that second, third, and fourth generation Puerto Ricans integrate themselves into mainstream society, and they move to more affluent neighborhoods, marry members of other ethnic groups, and become part of the 'American mainstream.' Their children are mainly English-speaking, and although they keep their Puerto Rican roots, they are not easily identifiable as Puerto Ricans. But they do not disappear as many writers tend to say. These days, Puerto Ricans are joined by brothers and sisters from other Latin American countries.

My roommate, Elbia was from San German, Puerto Rico. She was already settled in the tiny room. She was older than I was, and she was a faculty member of a private university in Puerto Rico. She was there on a faculty fellowship to upgrade her teaching skills by taking advanced graduate courses, and she continued to receive a monthly salary. She was in New York City mainly to take advantage of the multiple experiences provided by a cosmopolitan and culturally enriched urban environment. I asked her what she knew about the neighborhood or the services offered by the university to Latino students, and she responded:

"Angela, I do not know, and I am not interested in knowing what is going on beyond the walls of this place. I am not interested in finding out if there are other Latino students in this university or who the Puerto Rican leaders of the city are. I am not interested in knowing what other Puerto Ricans live in New York City or what they are doing."

"Why not?" I asked.

"Because that is not going to help me to take and pass my courses." Elbia said.

"But don't you feel that as Puerto Ricans, we should find out how other Puerto Ricans are doing in this university and throughout the city?" I asked.

"No," she said. "What should be important for you is to perfect your knowledge of the English language and make sure that your professors like you. Make sure you pass your courses with a satisfactory grade. Beyond that, the business of Puerto Ricans should not be your concern. That is not going to help you at all in this university."

And, at that moment, I realized that I was alone in this new city and in this new campus and that I needed to go ahead alone.

I always remember a dream I had while I was staying at the university dorms in the first month of my doctoral studies. One night while I was sleeping, I got out of bed, and I almost opened the door of the room, carrying with me two pillows, simulating two suitcases. My roommate Elbia asked me:

"What are you doing?"

I said, "I am going to Puerto Rico."

My roommate, half asleep laughed and said:

"Oh, no, you are not; you are going back to bed."

And I went back to sleep. The next day, I told my roommate that I was missing my family and my Puerto Rico. I was homesick, and if given the opportunity, I would return to the emotional comfort of Puerto Rico.

I was able to survive my first week in New York City. By the second week, I had attended all my classes, visited several offices of the university inquiring about part-time jobs for graduate students. The answer was: " No jobs available." I was aware that I was 30 years old, a woman, and a Puerto Rican from Puerto Rico. I came to the understanding that I was attending a private, upper class, white/Anglo university. When visiting the career and employment office, I went with the belief that everyone is treated the same, equal. I did not realize that I have a Spanish accent and that I am dark. The secretaries in the various offices shaped their hands into cones and put them over their ears when I talked to them, an indication that they did not understand what I was saying.

The white students never wanted to acknowledge that I was taking the same classes that they were taking. They talked to each other, and on occasion, when I tried to be part of the conversation, they did not acknowledge me- it was as if I did not exist. But I tried not letting them know how I felt. When in small groups, I would put my ideas on the table as if *"aquí no ha pasado nada "*(nothing has happened here). My peers' faces became tense and irritated. However, none of their behaviors stopped my involvement in the conversation. I looked at my situation, and I said to myself:

"I came all the way from Puerto Rico and made a lot of sacrifices to study here. I have faced so many challenges, and no one is going to stop me from getting this degree, not even my classmates. I need to study with hope and determination."

That first semester, I was taking an Educational Psychology class. The professor, Dr. Elias, (not his real name) assigned two textbooks with identified chapters to be read for each week of the class meetings. In each class, Dr. Elias used the same strategy over and over.

"Ok, class, discuss amongst yourselves the following: What new information do the assigned chapters present?" Dr. Elias asked every week.

"Ok, class, summarize on your own what you have learned. I will see you next week," Dr. Elias directed the class for the second time.

That was the professor's teaching activity every week. I felt very uncomfortable with this method.

"I would rather get the new information from him than from my peers," I thought.

My peers probably were like me, looking to get the main concepts and ideas from the assigned chapter. How different was this psychology professor from my high school teachers, especially Mr. Díaz, and from my professors from the Department of Pedagogy at the University of Puerto Rico! My professors in Puerto Rico provided a series of lectures about what they knew about the topic and, what they thought, we collectively needed to know. But here, in New York City, in this college, and especially in this class, we, the classmates, had to figure it out on our own. I was confused by Dr. Elias's method of teaching since many of the members of my group did not read the textbook chapters, and all they did in the group was talk about their jobs, their teaching, administrative issues, or personal problems. *Para colmo de males* (to make things worse), the professor informed us that the assessment of the course was going to be based on two multiple choice question exams and a final written research paper. The exams were based on the interpretation of the content of the text. I always read all the assigned readings for the weekly class meetings, and I knew the content but I never heard the professor explain his interpretation of the content of the chapters.

"How can I take and pass these two exams?" I thought.

In writing the final research paper, I never received guidelines or an outline to follow. What a difference from my professors from Puerto Rico! My professors in Puerto Rico gave me the topic and gave me specific guidelines to follow when writing the paper. The final paper that I wrote was on a topic that was familiar to me: *Qualities of Effective and Successful Teachers*. I never received the paper back, although I requested it several times from the professor.

I did not know how to handle this psychology professor; I was not getting the content of the course on my own. I needed someone to help me reflect and interpret the content of the book on a higher level. I did not need to be in a group of classmates who knew less than I did. I went to see the professor several times; he talked to me while he checked his mail or talked on the phone. He never looked at me, but concentrated more and more on his mail or phone conversation.

"You are doing fine," Dr. Elias said.

"No, I am not. I am lost," I said.

But he did not even know who I was or what my name was. I thought that he was not really interested in me as a person or as a student of his. I did not understand what this professor wanted from me as a student, and I could not get any information from him.

I struggled through this class. The professor gave me a low passing grade. I tried to meet with him to contest the grade, but I was never able to see him. He was always too busy for me.

I almost quit my doctoral program. But, after several days of crying and reflection, I learned from this experience that academic life was hard and sometimes, there was no fairness or justice. This professor taught me to work hard, perhaps, harder than anyone else of my peers in order to get whatever I had projected to accomplish. And I put that thought and attitude to work; I did not let anything or anyone, especially this psychology professor, put me off of what I planned to do in New York City, which was to get my doctorate.

The sky was gray and blue, light was coming out from the clouds, and the air smelled of spring. One of issues in this initial college experience in New York City was the constant sense of loneness. I was very lonely. Even when I was surrounded by people, I felt profoundly alone, and my roommate was in her own world. We almost never saw each other. I found that, although people surrounded me, I had no one to talk to. And, even when I tried to start a friendship, people were not willing to include me as part of the 'close friends.' I found a small group of Latino college peers, most of them enrolled in a master's degree program. I thought that I could count on them, however, I found that they were part-time students and were "too busy" to get involved in issues affecting Latino students. This group talked to me in a very superficial tone and was not really motivated to get involved in improving the conditions of Latinos in the university community. Our relationship did not go beyond seeing each other at the library or in the elevator.

During my two years in this doctoral program, this dark skinned, curly haired *jibarita* was not able to make or have social friends in the city. I found that most women were indifferent towards me. However, as lonely as I was, I always thought that I had to go ahead, to make it in New York City. I kept telling myself:

"The college, the city, and its surroundings are very hostile; but I have no choice, I have to go ahead. I have to make it in New York City."

I do not know if today, given the same circumstances, and with the same experiences that I had had, if I would have done something similar to what I did; which was to survive in a cold and hostile city and academic educational setting.

But there is always an angel in the path of every individual, and my angel was my adviser, an Argentinean man who valued and believed in me. My adviser, Santiago Luppoli, who later on became my mentor, was always giving me comfort and "ganas" to continue my struggle at the university. Because of his encouragement, I survived the first four months in the city of cold and snow.

"*Ud. está trabajando muy bien.* (You are doing fine.) Start preparing your doctoral dissertation proposal," he would say to me.

These were Dr. Luppoli's initial comments that greatly motivated me to continue to do my academic work. He believed in me and constantly acknowledged my academic preparation and ability. He even invited me to cover his classes when he had to attend a conference outside the city. Dr. Luppoli's encouragement was medicine for my soul.

A Hispanic Woman Who Makes a Difference: A Voice for English Language Learners with Communication Differences and/or Disorders

Linda I. Rosa-Lugo

Professor Linda I. Rosa-Lugo has been distinguished as *"a Hispanic Woman Who Makes a Difference."* Heralding from the Soundview Projects in the South Bronx in New York City, her journey to the academy did not follow a speedy or traditional route. Instead, she wound her way through a variety of teaching, administrative, and clinical side roads, all of which provided the firm foundation that underpins her teaching, research, and service in the academy. Her research focuses on understanding the social, linguistic and cultural needs of English language learners (ELLs) and the implications for speech –language pathologists (SLPs). Her research interests include dialect acquisition and usage in culturally and linguistically diverse students (CLD), language and literacy development in Hispanic youngsters who are deaf/hard of hearing, and first and second language acquisition in English language learners.

As a young child she was diagnosed with "Bell's Palsy" that resulted in a "communication disorder". Her interest in working with children with special needs stems from this personal experience and the rigorous course of rehabilitation she received in New York City's public schools and in clinical settings well into adulthood. This was the impetus for her to be "the voice" for individuals who experienced challenges in communication, and specifically for ELLs in the public school system.

Professor Rosa-Lugo completed her grade school education in the public schools of New York City, then graduated from St. John's University with a baccalaureate in Elementary Education with a minor in Speech-Language Pathology. She began teaching general education in a parochial school, but soon realized that she wanted to specialize in working with ELLs with special needs. She was a Title VII recipient at St. John's University and graduated with her masters' degree in Elementary Education with a specialization in Bilingual Education. She worked as a teacher in the New York City public schools.

As an educator in the New York City public schools, Professor Rosa-Lugo worked as a general and special education teacher, merging these interests to work in the first bilingual special education classes in New York City. She assisted in creating model curriculum for bilingual special education classrooms and worked with key individuals to promote bilingualism for children with special needs. She assumed a variety of administrative roles, however it was her first role as an Assistant Chairperson in a specialized assessment unit for children with sensory impairments, which led her to pursue doctoral studies in deafness. She continued in administrative positions in the New York City Board of Education, ultimately merging her interests and expertise in all areas of instruction: general, bilingual, and special education.

Throughout her professional career in New York City, she attended Teachers College, Columbia University and graduated with a Doctoral degree in Deafness. She continued her post-doctoral studies to obtain her Certificate of Clinical Competency in Speech-Language Pathology. Professor Rosa-Lugo obtained clinical experience (e.g., Harlem Hospital; New York Eye and Ear Hospital) working with individuals with communication disorders across the life span. Then she relocated to Florida where she worked in the public schools as a speech-language pathologist and ultimately in the academy.

Professor Rosa-Lugo is an associate professor at the University of Central Florida, Department of Communication Sciences and Disorders. Her publications have focused on dialect acquisition and usage in CLD students, language and literacy development in Latino children, and first and second language acquisition in ELLs. She is currently working on a book on language and literacy development for ELLs and is currently focusing her research on listening, language and literacy development in Latino children with cochlear implants.

Dr. Rosa-Lugo has been a Fulbright Scholar, is an active member of the national organization, The American-Speech-Language-Hearing Association (ASHA), serves as a consultant to the public school system, is a frequent speaker at national and international conferences and has been recognized as a *Hispanic Woman Who Has Made a Difference*.

You Will Not; You Cannot

You will not cry in front of a problem
getting up immediately, even if you fall again
full of hopes, happiness, and determination,
enthusiastically dreaming, without losing the fire.

You cannot stay still without a daily fight
taking responsibility for your own decisions.

You will not, you cannot show persistent anger
powerfully resisting dark and obscure forces.

You will not leave your own friends alone
without being appreciative that you have them,
and only calling them when the need arises.

You cannot forget people who love you
hiding on your own difficulties and egocentric attitude
forgetting to plant as many possible seeds
without love, your life cannot be complete.

You cannot stay in a fearful world
surrounded by lies and dishonest people
compromising integrity in narrow and small paths.

You will not live without forgiving your sister
even if a brother offended you several times,
you need to smile at the successful situation,
enjoying the journey, not only the final destination.

Chapter 6

ONE DAY AT A TIME

My husband, realizing that my doctorate was a long term endeavor, communicated to me his decision of quitting his job in Puerto Rico to move to New York City with the three children. And by the end of May, he, with our five and six year old sons boarded the *quiriquiquí*, a cheap late night flight from San Juan to Kennedy Airport. He carried on the plane all the personal belongings that he could: clothing, shoes, a small TV, a toaster, a radio, and dishes- and headed to New York City. My mother-in- law stayed with our infant daughter in Puerto Rico until we were settled in the City.

With many difficulties, I was able to rent a rat and roach-infested apartment in the "sures" of Brooklyn, which is today, a very desirable and expensive area. This is the only apartment I was able to find, after calling or visiting about twenty agencies and landlords.

Tío Chago, same uncle who brought me from Philadelphia to New York City, was generous enough to go to Kennedy airport to wait for my family. Tío Chago did not invite me to go to the airport since it would have been an additional trip from Philadelphia to Brooklyn, and then from Brooklyn to Kennedy Airport in Queens. That night, without being able to sleep, I waited for them in that unwelcome apartment. My family arrived to the Brooklyn apartment around 5 AM. A drop of sewer water in the front door welcomed them to the reality and challenges of living in New York City. Tío Chago, used to the poor conditions of Puerto Ricans in the United States, did not say anything. He just smiled. My two sons had so much hope and happiness that they did not mind the difficulties of getting wet at the entrance of the apartment building. My husband had too many things in his head to be preoccupied with drops of water. We were together and that was what mattered.

But the following three summer months were really difficult for the four of us. It was June, and I enrolled in the university summer program because the main purpose of being in New York City was for me to get this desired degree. I wanted to do it as quickly as possible. We had no jobs, and no money, and we were living in a miserable apartment. My husband immediately started to look for any available job in schools. In every place that he asked for a job, he was told:

"Sorry, *Señor*. We have no available jobs. As a matter of fact, we are letting people go because their jobs were eliminated to comply with the City call to decrease the current budget."

That was in 1973, when the City of New York was almost bankrupt, and many people were laid off. After a month of looking for jobs, my husband was ready to accept a job in a factory for a minimum wage salary starting late at night. And the same day that he was going to start this factory job, the New York City Board of Education offered him a job as an itinerary staff developer in a federally funded program.

"What a relief! Now, we will have money to pay the rent and buy food," I thought.

It was the beginning of July, and we started to look for a better apartment. And, with a job and salary, we were able to find an apartment at Church and Erasmus streets in Brooklyn. It was a comfortable apartment in a neighborhood under transition-white people leaving, and Latinos and blacks moving in. We moved on Labor Day because we needed to find a school for the two boys the next day- the first day of school for New York City public school students. On Labor Day, my husband rented a small U-Haul truck to move our few belongings to the new apartment. He put the mattresses on the top of the van, and began crossing the Eastern Parkway without noticing that the Annual African Caribbean Festival was passing through this avenue. No one could cross the avenue until the parade ended.

"*¡Oye, boricua, que carroza tan linda llevas!*" (Hey, Boricua, you have a beautiful carriage!"), a Latino yelled to my husband, who was waiting in the small truck for the caravan to end so that he could cross the avenue. Ah, the realities of New York City!

The next day, a September day, I took my two sons to school to enroll them in the neighborhood public school.

"We came from Puerto Rico two months ago," I said to the school receptionist. "What did you say?" she said very loudly, looking at the papers in front of her.

"My children do not know English. Do you have a bilingual program in which they can be placed?" I asked her.

"No, we do not teach in Spanish here. Everyone needs to learn and use English, which is the language of this country," the receptionist coldly said.

"Do you know if there is a school nearby that has a bilingual program?" I asked.

"No, and you are not entitled to enroll your child in another school, only here," the receptionist continued to put me down.

"This is the school that your children belong to, and need to attend. They must learn English, and they will only learn English when enrolling in a classroom where all the instruction is in English. Lady- this is not Puerto Rico."

I enrolled one of my sons at the school. My other son, who was five, was put on a waiting list because all of the half-day kindergarten classes were full.

"What did you learn in school today?" I asked my oldest son when he came back from school that afternoon.

"Well, I did what other children were doing. If they painted, I painted. If they opened a book, I did the same," my son responded.

"What did the teacher say?" I asked him.

"She did not come to my seat. She went around but never stopped in front of me," he said.

Tears ran from my eyes. My son did not understand a word of what the teacher was saying. The teacher did not care if he understood or not. She ignored him the whole day. But my son was intelligent enough to find a strategy to survive that unfriendly and unwelcome classroom and school environment. My husband and I started calling the few educators we had met during the last three months, inquiring about bilingual programs. *Bendito sea Dios*! (Bless God!) One week later, we found a bilingual program that was willing to take our two kids. It was a trilingual school-English, Spanish, and Haitian Creole- with a super bilingual educator as the supervisor. We took them to school and when they came back, their faces reflected happiness and learning. I knew that I had found the perfect school for my children. They attended this bilingual school (English, Haitian Creole, and Spanish) for one and a half years. This was a small well-run school where my sons performed very well, socially and academically.

I started to look for jobs in New York City but I was not able to find one. Weeks passed and we continued to struggle in New York City. But again, we had ganas, and we never looked back and stopped to think about how difficult these struggles were. We kept looking ahead!

Through the Migration Division of the Department of Labor of Puerto Rico in New York City, I found a job in the Puerto Rican Association for Community Organization (PACO), a community-based organization in Jersey City, New Jersey, as director of a small after school program. In addition to learning about educational issues, poverty and community issues, I gained experience supervising programs. This agency had received a federal grant to provide after school services to public school students. It was the first time that PACO was offering this type of program; therefore, the leadership of this organization looked upon me to plan and lead all aspects of the program. I, with the help of a co-worker, went to the Jersey City public schools to meet the principals and encourage them to recommend the PACO tutoring services to parents and their children. I tried very hard to motivate parents to bring their children to receive remedial reading and math as well as Latino cultural enrichment.

While at PACO, I continued working toward my degree, especially in the writing of my doctoral dissertation. I had already decided to write about three Puerto Rican sociologists and writers: Salvador Brau, Federico Degetau, and Manuel Fernández Juncos, to describe their influence, through their writings, on the educational system of Puerto Rico. Today, given my experience, I probably would have written about three Puerto Rican women. But then, I was focused on the main reason and purpose for leaving my comforts of Puerto Rico to come to New York: to get my doctorate in education so that when I returned to Puerto Rico to the college I left, I could have the same academic privileges and status as Dr. Smith and Professor Martínez.

I had completed one year directing the PACO program, but I was not happy with the direction that the program was taking. Students were not coming on a regular basis and the remediation was not related to students' school's academic curriculum. So, I decided to look for a different job in New York City.

My two-year-old daughter had just joined us. My mother-in-law had brought her from Puerto Rico, and she decided to stay with us for a couple of months until we were a little more stable. A year earlier, two months after my family moved to New York City, my mother had come with the idea of staying with us and helping with the three children. And she came to live with us, however, she could not deal with the inhospitality of the people, the language barrier, and the absence of her other children and family, and, three weeks later, went back to Puerto Rico.

I worked at PACO for a year, and then I left and found a part-time job. I worked as an administrative assistant one day a week (in a staff development program) at the headquarters of the New York City Department of Education. So, for about three or four months, I coordinated all clerical activities for the weekly staff development program that provided teacher training to assistant teachers (paraprofessionals). I was in charge of making sure that rooms were available, that supplies were in each room, and that participants' attendance was recorded. I had the opportunity to interact with different types of educators including the program director, the staff developers, the paraprofessionals, the secretaries, even with the custodian. Although this clerical job was only one day a week and not very challenging, it gave me the opportunity to familiarize myself with the New York City public school system. At every opportunity I had, I questioned the trainers as well as the paraprofessionals about schools, teacher recruitment, and types of students, school curriculum, and educational policies. It was at this place that I was informed of a supervisory job opening in a public school in the Bronx. One of the trainers told me of the immediate availability of a supervisory job.

"I just found out that there is a job available in a school in the Bronx," I mentioned to my supervisor, Angela Rosario-Basley.

"They are looking for an individual with a New York State supervisory license," my supervisor replied.

"I am licensed in the state of New York," I answered. (it was one of the first things that I did when I arrived in New York City). "Would you please do me a favor and call the school for me, and find out more about this job? I need to know how I can get in touch with the principal of the school. I want to apply for this job," I said to my supervisor.

My supervisor liked me, and she said that she would find out about the job. A week later, she called me up to inform me that the school district had received a federal grant, and part of the funding was used to pay for the salary of a bilingual supervisor at this school. The individual who had the job, a Puerto Rican woman, was promoted to principal of the same school, and they were looking for a qualified individual to fill her position. Because I had received my New York State teacher and supervisory license, I had the qualifications to apply for the job.

I applied, and I was immediately called for an interview. I was hired the same day of the interview as an elementary bilingual supervisor. This was a temporary supervisory job with a teacher's salary. At that time, because I was more concern about getting a full-time job, I did not care too much about getting a supervisory salary. I was told that the position would be available for as long as the grant would pay the salary.

It was the last week of December, and I put the few things we had in boxes. My husband, my three children, and I moved from Brooklyn to the Bronx. Unfortunately, I had to withdraw my two sons from that wonderful Brooklyn Bilingual Program.

I moved to what was and still is called the Soundview area in the southeast part of the Bronx. Looking for information about this borough, I read that the name of the borough, "*Bronx*," was taken from its largest and most important river, the Bronx River. This river received its name from a European colonist, Jonas Brock. From Brock came Bronx. I also read that the Bronx was a beautiful borough; with many unique areas, five universities, great parks, historical places, and residential areas. Soundview, the area that I was moving to, was a working community with a linguistic and ethnic mixture, notable for the Puerto Ricans who bought two-family homes, so they could rent an apartment to help pay for mortgage. We rented an apartment in one of those two-family homes.

Soon after I moved to the Soundview area, I found that there were many supermarkets in my neighborhood that were owned by Latino entrepreneurs and had been in existence for years. *El Guapo*, for example, not too far from Castle Hill Avenue, was a large loft where you could find almost every Latino product, in addition to the regular ones found in every supermarket. The best *recao, ajíes dulces, tayotes, achiote, ñames and malangas* are found, not in Puerto Rico, but in the Bronx. These products look fresh, as if they were taken from a nearby harvest. And they are also cheaper in the Bronx than in Puerto Rico. I love to go to the stores and get all the ingredients for the December 24th dinner *pasteles*; ingredients like: *yautía, plátanos, yuca, calabaza, guineos, madre de yautía, hojas de guineos*, and the string to tie the *pasteles*. Although most of these supermarkets were either Cuban or Dominican-owned, now they are mostly owned by Pakistanis and Indians.

Soundview was scattered with bodegas which in the 60s, 70s and 80s were mostly owned by Puerto Ricans, until the Dominicans began to establish their own. In these *bodegas* (small grocery stores), you can find almost anything: batteries, ice cream, rice, *bacalao*/codfish, sandwiches, coffee, newspapers, aspirin, and even antibiotics. Yes, *bodegas* sell every product under the sun!

Seeing them every day, I began to develop a sense of respect and admiration for the owners of these *bodegas*. Usually, they were managed by a married couple and their children. They were always so strong-willed and, in spite of not mastering the English language, they had the stamina to make it in New York City. Their *bodegas* opened around 4 AM and closed between midnight and 2:00 AM. In fact, some of these bodegas never closed. These families had to go to the wholesales outlets such as Hunts Point and the South Bronx Market to buy their products. They also had to make sure that the storefront was immaculate, because the city supervisor loved to give summons for not cleaning the front of the store. What an easy way for the city to increase their funds! Amazingly, the buildings next to the bodegas- houses, churches, or other buildings that did not clean their sidewalk fronts were never summoned. These *bodega* owners worked day and night, and in spite of the hard working conditions, they always appeared friendly and communicative.

I began working in the South Bronx, in an elementary school located near Westchester Avenue and 163rd Street, and I enrolled my two sons in the same school. I started as a Bilingual Education Supervisor. My daughter was enrolled in the Puerto Rican Association for Community Affairs (PRACA) Center, an early childhood program in the Castle Hill Avenue.

I had heard repeatedly that my new workplace was "a difficult school." Initially, I did not know what I was supposed to do, and no one was able to tell me what to do. I had never worked in a public school in the United States, and I did not know how business was conducted in the New York City schools. Although I had the supervisory license, I had never been an administrator, a principal or a supervisor in Puerto Rico. I asked the principal several times to describe my role and responsibilities as a bilingual school supervisor. The principal sat with me several times but never finished the conversation. Informally and through conversations with others who unexpectedly came to her office, I found that I was in charge of 50 percent of the students of the school - those who were enrolled in the Bilingual Program. Of these students, half were African Americans and half were Latino. I had to run all aspects of the "School Annex," a building with about 400 students who were enrolled in a dual language/two-way bilingual program.

Both groups of students, English proficient students and Spanish proficient, received instruction through English and Spanish. The difference between both groups was that the English proficient students received Spanish as a Second Language and the limited English proficient students received English as a Second Language. I had no idea how the program was supposed to be run, which subjects were supposed to be taught in Spanish and which ones in English. I had never taught African American students, so I did not know about their learning styles, cultural characteristics, and/or parents' preferences. I was totally blind. The only thing I knew was that I had to run this "mini school." The school had an assistant principal who never came to the annex; he was always in the main building. When I asked him for information or guidance, he interrupted me by saying:

"I am not responsible for the Annex. I do not work in the Bilingual Program."

During my first days in the school, I had a sincere desire to succeed and be useful. I did everything the principal said that I was supposed to do: I was in charge of discipline; I had to do daily lunchroom coverage while my 400 students were there. I observed teachers teaching, and I provided staff development to teachers and teacher assistants. Later on, the same teachers informed me that legally, I was not allowed to observe them because, officially, I was not a supervisor. Only principals and assistant principals were allowed to observe teachers. The lunchroom was a daily nightmare for me- all discipline issues came to me- I was policing all students. Neither the principal nor the assistant principal ever went to the lunchroom. Later on, I found that as a teacher assigned to temporary supervisor, I did not have to do lunch duty every day.

One of the biggest problems of the school was students' behavior, and I did not have the knowledge or the authority to deal with these behavioral problems. Every time there was a conversation with the principal about a student, she made me understand that, usually, it was not due to the student's behavior but to a lack of understanding of the student's culture and language by the teachers and the supervisory staff. There were teachers that could not control the students, so they called me for help. Since I did not know which my responsibilities were, I went to "calm" the students. And, most of the time, these students ignored me since they knew I had no authority. I spoke with the principal several times, and she assured me that I was doing a good job, and that I needed to relax a little bit. I tried to take it easy but I kept thinking that I needed to do more to help the teachers, the students, and the principal.

To make things worse, at 3 PM, when classes were dismissed, I was required to complete two additional hours at the district office under the supervision of my other supervisor, a Puerto Rican woman who was district supervisor in charge of Bilingual Education and who was in charge of the federal grant. The district office was about 20 minutes away by car. I asked my district supervisor if I could stay at my school to complete my daily schedule since I had so much paper-work to do, and she said:

"No, you cannot. It is the district's regulations that staff that are paid by federal funds need to put in two additional hours of work daily. And I have decided that those extra hours of work be at the district office, where I can supervise the entire group of supervisors involved. We will use these two hours for meetings, to buy supplies, or for other needs of the grant," she said.

Again and again, I spoke with the district supervisor trying to convince her to allow me to stay at the school.

"You must come to the district office every day and punch the time card to verify that you were here. Your check comes from this office," she repeated to me several times.

So, every day, at 3:30 PM, I drove to the district office, usually arriving around 4:00 P M, where I spent an additional hour at the district office. But I made sure that I was there every school day, and I made sure that I signed the daily attendance sheet and punched the time card.

Two months passed after being hired as an elementary bilingual supervisor. I struggled every day, but as weeks passed, I felt that I was adapting to the culture and demands of the school, although, I was not satisfied with my accomplishments- I was merely surviving day by day. There were not too many major things happening, through every day was a hectic one, with paper-work, discipline issues, and teachers' need for staff development and training.

One day, the principal sent me a written note to the School Annex. The note said:

"This is very important; come immediately to the main office."

I walked very quickly from the School Annex to the principal's office. When I arrived at the office, the principal was accompanied by two employees from the South Bronx Parents Association, a community- based organization that mainly offers day care and after school programs for children. The organization was founded by the renowned Evelina Antonetti. Antonetti was an institution in the South Bronx- very well- respected, admired, loved, and feared. To be honest, I had never heard of the South Bronx Parents Association or of Evelina Antonetti, therefore, I had no idea what the purpose of the meeting was, and why I had to participate in such a dialogue.

The principal introduced the two ladies to me, and then she provided me with a short introduction of the South Bronx Parents Association and its powerful influence in the community, in the school, and in the Bronx school districts. The ladies mentioned that the main function of the South Bronx Parents Association was to assure quality education for children of the neighborhood as well as services provided for parents to help their children at home and at school.

"We want to meet you because we have a message for you. We like the Bilingual Education District Supervisor who we presently have at the district level. We support her, and we want her to stay in that position," they told me.

"I do not understand what is going on here," I said.

"You came here yesterday, and we heard that you are interested in getting the district Bilingual Education Supervisor's position. We want you to know that we are happy with the person that we already have."

"We love her, and we want to keep her," they repeatedly said.

"Do you understand what we are telling you?" they pressed.

At that time, for the first time in my short time in New York City, I began to understand the politics and survival of the South Bronx. People protected themselves against anyone who comes from the outside.

"I am not interested in anyone else's job. I want to keep this job," I only said. "But we are also involved in who gets this job permanently. We are not saying that you cannot apply, be interviewed and hired," the two visitors emphasized.

After that, the conversation turned to Puerto Rico, where I had lived, and why I had decided to come to the Bronx.

The principal did not say anything; she just smiled and agreed with what they were saying. She did not say anything on my behalf, nor did she comment on what the two visitors were mentioning. She performed very well in her role of convening the meeting. And I thought to myself that she probably went to them too when she applied for the principal's position at the school.

That night, I was awake all night thinking about what had transcended that day.

And from that day on, I was very careful in what I said to the people around me. Although I was starting to be accepted in the school, I realized that my supervisor career was not going to continue in that school or in that district. After that, I became very careful with my district supervisor. I did not tell her about the conversation with the staff of the South Bronx Parents Association, nor did she ask me about it, although I realized that she knew everything that was going on. This conversation gave me the motivation to work hard to finish my doctorate.

I was almost done with my dissertation research, and I made the decision to move up in my life. I worked late nights in order to finish the document. When the day of the dissertation oral defense came, I told my principal and my district supervisor of the need to be absent that day. I did not tell them that I was going to the university for my oral dissertation examination. However, I had been able to get the confidence and acceptance of most of the teachers of the school. So, informally, I had mentioned them that I had completed my doctoral dissertation, and I had scheduled the oral defense that week. And, when I went back to school the next day, the teachers, at lunchtime, had prepared a social gathering for me with food, a ceremony, and a flower corsage. The teachers were very happy about my academic accomplishment. I think that the principal was also proud of a Puerto Rican *jibarita* from her school, receiving a high educational achievement.

How I finished my doctorate in a short period of time is still a mystery to me, especially when I had very little resources available and limited time due to my role as a mother, wife, and full-time or part-time worker. But again, the help of my adviser and my *ganas* were always there. My desire "to make it" was my strongest force. I made every possible effort to alleviate cultural, language, learning, and financial barriers by having a positive attitude every time that I approached a difficulty. What drove me to succeed were the *ganas, ganas, and* more *ganas*: to make it in New York City.

At the end of the day, when I went to the district office, my dress showed the orchid corsage that my colleagues had given me. I sat in the district office until the time expired, and I punched my card and left. No one congratulated me. I thought to myself:

"*A veces tu propia gente es tu peor cuña.*" (Sometimes, your own people are your worst enemy.)

I only spent six months (which seemed like several years) in that elementary school, as a bilingual education supervisor and with that school principal.

And, one month after receiving my doctorate diploma, I received a phone call from a private university in New York City that was interested in hiring me as a full-time professor of English as a Second Language and Bilingual Education. What an irony! I had had vast experience in teaching Spanish; however, this university was offering me a job in two fields for which I had no experience, outside of my supervisory position. Luckily, I took all my electives in *Teaching English as a Second Language,* and I came with a strong background in Spanish language and literature.

A Firm Advocate of Study Abroad and Multicultural Education

Amarilis Hidalgo de Jesús

Professor Amarilis Hidalgo de Jesús is a firm advocate of study abroad programs and multicultural education. Professor Hidalgo de Jesús completed her doctorate. in Latin American Literature at the University of Colorado, Boulder. She attended Temple University and the University of Puerto Rico, Río Piedras Campus for her M.A. studies in History and Spanish. She earned her baccalaureate degree in history from the University of Puerto Rico, Río Piedras Campus. In 1991 she accepted a teaching appointment at Northeast Missouri State University, and in 1992 moved to Bloomsburg University in Pennsylvania. Since then, she has taught at this university. She is currently a full professor of Spanish at that institution.

Professor Amarilis Hidalgo de Jesús directs Bloomsburg University's Study Abroad Programs to Spain and exchange programs in Spain and Puerto Rico. She has also coordinated internships in both countries and Mexico. Dr. Hidalgo de Jesús is an avid traveler as well. She has traveled, researched, and attended conferences in several European, North American, Latin American, and Caribbean countries. Her area of expertise has taken her to do research in Venezuela. She has also done research on Colombian, Cuban, Mexican, Puerto Rican, and comparative literature.

At Bloomsburg University, Professor Hidalgo de Jesús devotes much of her time to mentoring minority students and students who want to pursue studies abroad. She advises formally the international/national students from Spain and Puerto Rico, and she is also the informal advisor of other international students. She is the advisor of SOL (Students Organization of Latino). She is constantly organizing activities to bring diversity to Bloomsburg University and the community. She has also served as a liaison between the university community and the town. She devotes some of her time interpreting for migrant workers working in the area.

Besides being a server and a community leader, Dr. Hidalgo de Jesús has published three books, and several articles and book reviews. Among her most important publications are *La novela moderna en Venezuela; Escritura y desafío: Narradoras venezolanas del siglo XX; and Spain, Beyond Culture and Literature*. Profesor Hidalgo de Jesús is currently working on the project "*Narradoras, relatoras, cuentistas: Escritoras puertorriqueñas a partir de los años 80.*" She has completed a manuscript on Latinos in U.S. culture.

Professor Hidalgo de Jesús has presented numerous papers on Latin American literature and comparative literature at international, national, and regional conferences. Due to her area of research on Venezuelan literature, she has been invited to give lectures by several universities in Venezuela. She also has been awarded several research and cultural grants.

Latina Professor

I respect your many hours of academic dedication
your wisdom, ingenuity, humbleness, and sensibility
embracing languages as required learning
aggressive counselor of multicultural affairs
lectures full of knowledge, clarity and oracy
receiving from students a strong ovation.

Fighting ignorance and cultural illiteracy
confronting many, in providing intellectual knowledge
conquering difficult and ambiguous academic worlds
writing, speaking, teaching, demonstrating
always planting the idea, always planting the seed
traveling, to introduce, to share, and to receive
often surrounded by continuous and agitated controversy
especially coming within communities of resistance.

I give you flowers, especially my garden sunflowers
the delicious fruits that are rarely found
the best wine from the famous vineyards
and the best bread that I am able to find.
And in the same basket, I am happily putting
three classic books of Spanish literature
El Quijote, Mis Memorias, Cien Años de Soledad.

I give you thanks for what you are,
You are a Latina Professor.

Chapter 7

BEING THE CHANGE

Someone said:

> *"It is prohibited not to smile at the problems*
>
> *Not to work hard toward what you want,*
>
> *To abandon the struggling moments for fear of failing,*
>
> *Not to make your dreams realities.*

The academic world is a maze: the stairs to get to success go in several directions at the same time; they are arduous, painful, and often confusing. For Latinas, especially Latina professors, the journey is even harder, because there are very few colleagues in this academic world that you can call *"amigos"*. As I said before, at the final stage of my doctoral degree, I received a phone call from a professor who was working in a private university in New York City.

"This is Dr. RB. There is a position available at this university, and someone who knows you gave me your name as a possible candidate for the position. If interested, I encourage you to apply for this position," he said.

I was delighted to hear his invitation to apply. Remember, I had been in New York City for only 2 years! And, I had worked very hard for my degree. I made so many financial, family, and academic sacrifices to complete the doctoral program, especially finding the money to pay for the tuition at a very expensive private university. Reflecting back, I still do not know how I was able to start, and later, complete this degree. During those 2 years, I had worked in several jobs because I needed the money. I made the time to work, to study, and to be a mother, and a wife. I thought that this phone call was a sign of things changing for the better.

Without thinking twice, I told Dr. RB that I accepted his invitation and would apply for the position of professor at his university. I immediately sat at my electric typewriter and wrote a letter to the dean of the school, indicating my interest in the advertised posting of professor of English as a Second Language and Bilingual Education. And, although I applied for the job, I was totally convinced that I was not going to be called for an interview. One main reason was that when I was talking by phone to Dr. RB, inquiring about the demands and duties of the position, my heavy Spanish accent was evident. He asked me several times to repeat what I had said; giving me the impression that he did not completely understand everything I was saying. However, a few days later, I received a phone call from the university, inviting me for an interview. I said to myself: "Alleluia!"

When I arrived at the university, the same professor, Dr. RB, was waiting for me and said:

"Welcome! Bienvenida! "

This professor was very helpful and encouraging; he also stayed with me throughout the day, and he gave me the confidence to survive this new experience. He also showed me all the different offices of the university and introduced me to the people who worked in these offices. Today, when I see this professor, I always remind him of the difference he made that day by giving me the confidence and support to complete the long day of meetings and interviews.

The first interview of the day was in the nature of a group interview, where the assembled professors asked me questions about my academic knowledge and expertise. I remember some of those questions.

"Define the linguistic weaknesses of students for whom English is a new language," a female professor asked me, looking into my eyes.

"Which are the differences between teaching ESL (English as a Second Language) to children and teaching ESL to adults?" a male professor, sitting to my left, asked me.

"Which ESL methodologies do you use with students for whom English is not their first language?" another professor asked me, looking at a copy of my curriculum vitae that he held in his hands.

I had never taught English in United States schools, but I had observed and worked with teachers in Jersey City and in the South Bronx who were teaching students to become literate in English. I had taken courses in the teaching of ESL in my doctoral program. In addition, during my twelve years of schooling in Puerto Rico, I was an English as a second language learner myself. So, I was confident in how to teach English as a Second Language. In responding to the above questions, I stated all the knowledge I had gained through my teaching of Spanish in Puerto Rico, through the direct experience in the after school program in New Jersey, through my doctoral courses, and mostly, through those months in the south Bronx school. The professors listened to what I had to say, their face movements and smiles showed me that, in general, they were satisfied with my responses. This body language gave me the confidence to provide multiple examples and descriptions. I was satisfied with the way I answered all of the questions.

That day, I also met several administrators, department chairs, and several other professors from other academic departments. These individuals asked me detailed academic questions. One question that was repeated several times was:

"How prepared are you to enter the professorial world?"

With all the humility that I was able to muster, I reminded them that I was not new to academia, that I had two years of professorial experience in Puerto Rico. One of the senior professors said to me:

"But, Professor, remember, this is not Puerto Rico. This is the United States. This is New York City. If you are hired, you will be challenged by graduate students as well as by colleagues."

"With all due respect, let me say that in Puerto Rico, we too teach English as a Second Language, and Puerto Rican educators are familiar with the most recent theorists and methodologies in the field of education," I said. "Students in Puerto Rico have the advantage of learning content areas in Spanish, their first language, and at the same time, they learn English as a second language. These students are encouraged and taught to become bilingual. I think that they have an advantage over students in the mainland United States."

The room was silent, and I understood that the group was probably not aware of the educational reality of Puerto Rico and the Puerto Rican educational system.

At the end of the day, I met with the Dean of the School of Education. After he examined my academic credentials and teaching experience, and without looking at me, he asked me:

"Professor: who is going to take care of your three children?"

"I am making arrangements," I said.

"What type of arrangements?" he asked.

"I have a neighbor who will take care of my three children," I said.

And I outlined my plan for taking care of the children, making sure that he understood that my children would not interfere with my teaching job.

"I wish this man knew of all the jobs I had worked without the interference of my three children," I said to myself. "How often I have struggled to take the children to school or make miracles to have someone at home by the time the kids were arriving from school."

Still today, I wonder if this Dean asked the same type of questions to the other faculty candidates, especially to the male candidates, who were interviewed by him the same week. At that moment, I realized that this dean had a wrong idea about Puerto Ricans in general, and especially Puerto Ricans in the mainland United States. I did not say anything because I wanted and needed the job. I had to go along with answering whatever questions he asked me.

At the end of the week, the Dean's assistant called me up to tell me that he, the Dean wanted to see me again. By 3:30 PM the next day, I was in the Dean's office. He offered me the position, along with the lowest possible salary. I did not say "no" but I showed him a paper with the salary that I was making in the public school system. I told him that the salary I was receiving was much more than what he was offering me. He kept looking at the papers he had in front of him. He was in that position for probably 30 minutes without looking at me. Reluctantly, he offered me three thousand dollars more than the initial salary offer. I accepted.

In September, with a very low starting salary, an initial professorial rank, and a mere one year contract, I started my professorial journey in the United States. I became a full-time professor in the Graduate School of Education. Assistant professor is the lowest appointment rank that a professorial candidate can get after receiving a doctorate in a recognized field. I was the only Latina and the first Puerto Rican professor in the whole school of about 40 full-time faculty members. And, perhaps, the first Latina in the entire university.

The Dean of the School of Education, who was an educational historian and biographer of Horace Mann, was not enthusiastic about the appointment. Clearly, I was not "uno *de los santos de su devoción*" (one of his favorite saints). He did not give me the same treatment as the other professorial candidates he hired the same month. Everyone else hired received a two-year contract; however, I was hired for only one year. Why did he hire me, then? He was probably forced to.

Universities are always applying for grant monies from local, state, and federal organizations or institutions to supplement their own budget. At that time, the federal government was providing monies to train teacher candidates to pursue degrees in the field of bilingual education. This university was awarded a grant to pay college tuition for qualified bilingual teacher candidates for the duration of three years. However, the university had only one faculty in the area of bilingual education. Perhaps, in order to comply with the grant guidelines, the Dean hired me to expand his faculty members in the area of bilingual education. I was a viable candidate because I had some formal education and expertise in bilingual education, ESL and Spanish. I had a doctorate, I had experience as a supervisor, and I had teaching experience in Puerto Rico as well as some academic writing experience.

When I was hired, my first publication, a short book, *La Enseñanza de la Lectura en Español en la Escuela Elemental*, was in the process of being printed. This short book was written in Spanish while I was writing my doctoral dissertation. Writing this book in Spanish served as 'dissertation therapy' for me because I found pleasure in putting my ideas together beyond the monotonous doctoral methodology. Although this short book is not a highly complex book, it describes scenarios in the teaching of reading in Spanish and the prevalent methodologies of the 1970s. During that time, the majority of bilingual children in the mainland United States were Hispanics, so there was a need to prepare teachers in the teaching of reading through Spanish. When the Dean of the School of Education first interviewed me, I showed him the "galleys" that I had received from the publisher and the letter indicating the exact date of publication. I was proud of this book because it provided me with the opportunity and experience of writing in the academic world. However, the dean ignored the manuscript and continued to inform me about his expectations regarding my role and responsibilities.

After being in the university for several months, I discovered that one of the games of being a successful professor was to publish. "Publish or perish" was repeated to me several times. Thus, I spent a great deal of time writing in my field. I became interested in writing about bilingual education, English as a Second Language, as well as issues affecting the education of Puerto Rican/Latino children in the United States. I authored books and monographs alone, and with colleagues. I edited or co-edited several books. One in particular, *Hispanic Children and Youth in the United States* showcases the realities of many Latino children who are challenged by social, economic, linguistic, educational, and cultural struggles. *The Neo-Rican: Unwelcome in Two Worlds* touched me very profoundly. In this short monograph, I was able to describe the sad situation of many Puerto Rican children and youth who were born or raised in the United States and had to move with their parents to Puerto Rico. These children and youth are not welcome in Puerto Rico, mainly due to cultural and linguist differences.

It was not until the end of the first academic year that I found out that I was appointed in a "soft professorial line," which meant that the university had no responsibility towards me as a professor, not even with my salary, which was coming from an external funding source. The federal government had recently enacted the 'Title VII Bilingual Education Act,' and part of the funding was provided to teacher training programs to prepare qualified bilingual education teachers. And universities such as this one were taking advantage of the funding by hiring faculty with the credentials to teach in the area of bilingual education. I also discovered that I received a one-year contract only, while the rest of the professors hired that year received two-year contracts. When I questioned the academic department chair, he responded by saying:

"Go and ask the dean."

I insisted in continuing the conversation, although he would not.

"When I was interviewed for this job, it was not explained to me that this was a temporary job," I said. "I am inquiring about my future in this university."

The chair was not interested in pursuing the conversation or in giving me information related to my professorial contract. And I was afraid to speak to the Dean, the tall and enigmatic man, afraid that he would ask me for more details about how my children were taken care of while I was working at the university. So, I decided to find out through other professor colleagues the reality of professors who were not in tenure tract lines but in the insecure "soft lines."

I met with the more senior influential professors, to ask for guidance and advice. I asked them questions such as:

"Can you advise me on what I need to do to transfer from a soft line to a tenure track line? What steps do I have to take towards ensuring a better future for myself in this university?"

"Please be more specific," most of them said.

I made my requests more specific but some of them went further to say:

"Aren't you happy that you work here, even if it is in a soft teaching line? You have a job here for the rest of the time that the grant exists, and most grants have a five- year life."

Other colleagues were more diplomatic; they looked at me with indifference and pushed me out by saying:

"Sorry, I do not know the procedures used by the university or the dean in terms of hiring faculty. I wish I could be more helpful to you."

I went back to Dr. RB, who at the time was not a senior faculty but he was trying to work toward his tenure. He encouraged me by saying:

"Let's find out answers to your queries together. I need to meet with the dean to get his signature for a federal grant that I am submitting, and I will indirectly ask him about your situation."

He came back very discouraged.

"The dean did not want to discuss the issue with me," he said.

I did not stop questioning colleagues, and reminding the academic department chair about my concern regarding my situation.

I made the decision to go and confront the Dean. I had to wait a month to secure a meeting date with him. At the meeting, he almost did not let me speak but reminded me that I knew when I signed the contract; it was for one year to be paid by money generated by an external funding. He suggested that if I was not happy with the assignment, to resign at the end of the semester.

"I cannot do that; I like what I do here which is training teacher candidates. How about if, rather than giving me a one-year contract, you change it to two years?" I asked.

"I cannot do that," he said.

I left his office. Two months later, he informed the faculty that he was leaving the deanship to become president of a small university in Pennsylvania. I was neither happy nor sad.

When the new dean came, I was one of the first faculty members to meet with him and ask to change my contract. He looked at me and said:

"I cannot assure you anything, but I will look into the matter."

At that time, I realized that I had to start with small steps; first a two-year contract, and then the challenge was going to be to change from a soft line to a tenure track. It took many meetings with influential colleagues, and with the chair, to persuade the new dean to change my one-year contract to a two-year contract, particularly because my salary was coming from a multi-year funding source.

After two years of continued persuasion, I was able to receive a two-year contract. This new contract meant that I did not have to prepare reappointment papers every year, similar to the other four professors who were hired the same year that I was hired. While I was enjoying the victory of this battle, I was reminded of the possibility of being out of a job at the end of the grant period if the external funding was not renewed.

I then realized that I had to start the process of convincing my colleagues and the school administration to consider the idea of changing my faculty track status. The dean who hired me had left, but, my journey with the newly appointed dean had just begun. I met several times with him to explain that my academic credentials, my teaching experience and service merited a tenure track position. When I met with him, he looked at me and remained silent for a long time, and then said:

"Sorry, I have no tenure line to offer you. Those lines come from the Vice-President for Academic Affairs. The School did not receive approval for new tenure track lines this year."

I insisted and he always gave me the same response:

"I heard you but I do not have an authorized tenure track line to give you. I have told you several times that I cannot do that, but you don't seem to understand."

"I hear you, but I do not understand why you cannot ask for a new line," I said to the dean.

"There are no faculty lines available," the dean repeated again and again the same answer.

The last time that he said it, I left his office and I went to those few influential professors that had showed some interest in my situation, and I asked them to talk with other colleagues, with the chair and the dean on behalf of my case. I offered to work with them in committees, and in outside activities. I offered to do whatever they needed, and I attended all activities promoted by those influential professors. I also showed them the academic work that I was working on- publications, scholarly presentations, school staff development- to try to convince them to be in favor of my crusade. This journey took me one year.

Then, one day the dean called me back to his office and said:

"You will get a new contract. This contract is a two-year contract as a tenure track assistant professor."

I finally won the battle! I was moved to a tenure track position the same month.

Then I realized that I had only one year to prepare for tenure, and I had heard the horrible stories of colleagues whose tenure was denied. I was fearful of the process, but I knew that I had to confront this new battle. I reviewed my credentials, and although I was not totally confident, I was satisfied with the quality and quantity of my academic work, mainly the publications. These publications were researched and written while I fought for my two-year contract and my tenure track position. I also became familiar with most of the professional associations in my field, and I became an active member of each. And I made sure to meet several influential female professionals within the New York City Department of Education.

It was around this time that I had the good fortune to meet Aida. Aida was a charismatic New York City administrator, and later on, she became a school principal and a Pentecostal minister. I met her at the university where I was completing my doctoral program and later on, I went to her district to conduct staff development presentations. We became close and have maintained our friendship throughout the years. She is someone that I call to share ideas with and to talk to about social and educational issues. Aida is outspoken and pushy, and she speaks freely about anything and everyone, sometimes even in favor of issues or individuals that I do not agree with. However, I admire her honesty and she is a great human being with a high desire for sharing. Aida never ceases to surround people with gifts and dinner invitations, and any special treat that she knows will make an *amiga* happy. And, although we have completely different personalities, think differently, and have different opinions, we can spend a week together, and never tire of each other's company. I never told Aida about my work situation since there was nothing she could do. However, I did do several staff developments projects in the school district in which she worked. Through her, I met influential educators, I worked in a city-wide educational committee on gifted education, and together, we published an in-service monograph on gifted education for Latino students.

I was during my professorial battle, that I received the message that my mother was very sick. I went to Puerto Rico several times that year to visit and comfort her. However, her condition deteriorated and she never recovered. My children, my husband and I went to Puerto Rico on an emergency trip to say goodbye.

One year later, I applied for tenure. I was even more scared due to the pushing I had done to get a tenure track position. And, I was not even sure if this new dean was happy with having a Latina in his professorial group. One day, after my application for tenure was submitted, three colleagues from my department, the Department of Curriculum and Teaching, invited me for lunch. I was skeptical since they had never asked me to join them before.

"There is a group of colleagues who are not convinced by your academic scholarship, and they are not recommending you for tenure," the professors said to me while eating their BLTs.

I was aware of what they were telling me, and because I had seen the ambivalence of some of my colleagues toward my work, and toward me, I had made the decision early of publishing as much as possible. At the end of my fourth year at the university, I had already written two books and several articles. One of those books was written in Spanish on the topic of teaching reading in Spanish. The second book was a compilation of articles from several educators, written in English and Spanish. I had written the introduction and I contributed three articles, written in Spanish or English.

"Why did you write your first book in Spanish? We are in the United States, and a book that we cannot read is not going to be well-received," a colleague asked me while examining my tenure portfolio.

My colleagues could not wrap their heads around it- they had never confronted scholarly work in a language other than English. My colleagues had a difficult time accepting these publications as "scholarly work" because they did not read Spanish and the publishing companies (both located in Spain) were not known to them.

Tenure at colleges and universities has several steps and stages. At this university, the candidate is first recommended for tenure by the faculty of the school, and then recommended by the dean, then the University Tenure Review Committee, and the final decision is in the hands of the president of the university.

I heard that the meeting to recommend or deny me for tenure was a long one. As I was informed by a group of colleagues, a group of professors arduously argued against granting me tenure. Arguments included:

"Her books are written in Spanish, not in English."

"The editorial house of the Spanish book is an unknown one."

"Who are these people that wrote articles in the edited book? Do they exist?"

"Her articles do not deal with issues relevant to the general population."

In the end, my colleagues voted, and the majority of the group voted in favor of granting me tenure, in spite of the energetic argument presented by a minority group. The decision was then put in the hands of the dean. The dean, from I was told was ambivalent on what to do. Dr. RB, (who, at this time, was already tenured and participated in the meeting) met with the dean several times because he had heard that the dean was not sure about his decision of recommending or not recommending me for tenure. This professor urged him to look at the merits of the candidate, and not to listen to the recommendations of a small vocal group of professors.

After persistent persuading by a group of colleagues, the dean recommended my tenure. However, his letter of recommendation stated: "She is not a scholar and she will never be." But rather than being angry or bitter by the dean's statement, I used it as motivation to continue my academic journey.

The president granted me tenure. I was the first Latina, and the first Puerto Rican, to receive tenure in the Graduate School of Education at this university.

I continued to work hard and be motivated to continue the struggle within communities of resistance. I was promoted to associate professor, to professor, and four years before retirement, the president conferred me the honor of Distinguished Professor of Education. I would not have made it to this point were it not for a few core strategies that I continually turned to.

First, I tried not to become a "victim" of the system of the people surrounding me. I always used the struggles or failures or disappointment to motivate me to be a better person or a better professional. I truly believed that if I became the victim, would have I finished as a failure. I never confronted those colleagues that voted against my tenure though I saw them frequently. As a matter of fact, throughout the years, some of them became my friends, and others have collaborated with me in professional projects. I used their criticism as a foundation for personal growth and academic development.

Second, I never accepted "no" for an answer. Throughout my professorial journey, I kept asking questions, asking for explanations, reading the small print, and reminding people about my rights as a human being, as a woman, as an academician, and as a professor. I tried to do these things with professionalism and without insults or offenses. It really works.

Third, I kept academically active, and I continued to produce. Although other colleagues or peers told me not to do this or that, that I had done so much, I did not pay attention to these individuals, and I kept being involved in the field of teaching and learning. I did it with motivation, and in doing it, I felt a lot of satisfaction in what I had done.

Fourth, I used the negativity expressed by some of my colleagues as a tool of encouragement. Sometimes, colleagues who had worked next to me, and had known my work and my professional activities for many years, said things like:

"No puedo creer que esto lo hiciste tú." (I can't believe you did that) And every time they repeated this phrase, I looked at them and I said:

"Yes, believe it-I did it. "

I was aware of their meaning, intentional or not, but I took their words as encouragement to continue to work hard. Collectively, all these individuals have contributed to who I am today: a Puerto Rican female professor who feels satisfied with her professional journey. And this journey, though difficult, frustrating and disenchanting at times, has provided me with many, many rewards.

Teaching and those who value education are always high in my mind. Teachers and professors have the opportunity to provide generations of excellence. My journey has been blessed by the work of many successful and effective educators, specifically those from Puerto Rico, such as Juanita Méndez, Carmen Gómez Tejera, Concha Meléndez, and Rafael Cordero. Rafael Cordero, who at the end of the nineteenth century, and around a tobacco table, taught many poor children in Puerto Rico. Thanks to Cordero's dedication, persistence, and motivation, Puerto Rico produced some powerful individuals. Carmen Gómez Tejera, a Spanish teacher and professor who loved teaching, spent a great deal of time and energy providing staff development to other teachers. Juanita Méndez and Concha Meléndez are remembered as intelligent and dedicated teachers, professors, researchers and writers. It is because of dedicated teachers such as these that children, youth, and adults were, are, and will be prepared to assume responsibility as leaders.

I express my gratitude to those that are teaching today, to those that taught yesterday, to those teachers and professors that are now retired, and to those that have passed. I feel proud to be a pedagogue, and that I can be counted as part of those who have made so many efforts to improve the human race.

Leader in Web-Assisted Learning

Alma Abdel-Moty

Alma Abdel-Moty is known by her colleagues as "relentless;" her students call her "mother hen;" in her field she is known as the leader in web-assisted learning; and to her husband, she is "Mi Amor." Dr. Alma Abdel-Moty (born Alma Milagros Rivera) is an occupational therapist, professor, educator, a daughter, wife, and mother; in no particular order.

Alma is the Chairperson of the Occupational Therapy Department at Florida International University in Miami Florida. She graduated from the University of Puerto Rico in 1982 with a Bachelor of Science in Occupational Therapy.

Soon after, she joined the Vocational Rehabilitation Center in Río Piedras as a staff Occupational Therapist. What happened after that was not in her plans as the only child of Jose and Alga. Considering her sheltered life until the age of 24, Alma could not have imagined what life had in store for her when she interviewed for an OT position with the University of Miami Comprehensive Pain Center. As the story goes, recruiters from that Pain Center were in PR looking for therapists. "Why not?" she said to her girl friends who read the ad in the local newspaper. She went that morning to the interview, not knowing that in a few weeks she would get the phone call to pack and head to Miami. Fear. Uncertainty. Excitement. But again, why not?

"With a one-way ticket, I got on that plane after a heart-breaking "*A Dios que te bendiga*" from my parents," she recalls, not knowing that she was on her way to a brighter future. No doubt, she can still hear the pounding of her heart and the echoes of their heavenly prayers.

Life in Miami was different; yet similar. Being the cultural melting pot of South Florida, Miami was the perfect place for Alma. Although she felt very comfortable speaking English, many Miamians spoke only Spanish; whether from Cuba, Puerto Rico, Colombia, or Argentina. Other than missing her mother's arroz *con gandules*, food in Miami was pretty "homey." People were nice, but kept their distance. That period of adjustment did not last long as she immersed herself in work while she tried to settle down in a small apartment in Hialeah.

People of the Pain Center were very supportive and welcomed the new arrivals from Puerto Rico. With one in particular, she felt immediate connection. Eight months later they were married; and still are after 25 years. Alma went on to get her Masters degree in Occupational Therapy (OT), began teaching at FIU, got her Doctorate in OT and became the successful, hard-working Puerto Rican she now is.

"Excellence in teaching, in advising, and at work" was and still is her motto. Alma earned several teaching awards, for embedding cutting edge technology in web-assisted courses. She added video clips and voice-over to her interactive learning, and entered exclusive teaching competitions. She advised students by designing course sequences for "off track" students, reviewing SASS reports, and reviewing graduation certifications.

Alma's focus on personal growth and professional development are paramount to her success. She participates in conferences, courses, and workshops to enhance her teaching skills and to further develop her professional competencies. She works with community organizations, and she opened her students' minds and experiences to technological advancement.

Even though Alma is considered a force in leadership and mentorship, she found administrative tasks and assignments a lesser favorite. Driving by dignity, compassion, and respect, she worked diligently with teams of colleagues to develop new courses that aim for higher levels of excellence. Putting her own interests aside, Alma has provided extensive support to faculty members in their effort to seek funding, promotions, or networking. She is committed to seek resources, facilitate networking opportunities, and strategize through her "animated" Latin ways of communicating and conveying a message.

Meeting the expectations of those who work with Alma posed yet another challenge; and an opportunity. She was expected to mobilize the faculty towards increasing scholarship activities and submission of extramural research grants. She was also expected to mentor and support junior faculty in their research, finalize and obtain approval for new curriculum, increase students' national examination pass rates, and coordinate faculty input and feedback in designing new facilities. All constituted imagination, persuasion, and a little bit of good luck. She met and exceeded those expectations to improve the quality and rigor of the academic experience.

Whether it was her passion for being an occupational therapist, or her instinct as a nurturing Puerto Rican female, Alma's role as a mother and a wife did not suffer. She had a daughter, Karima, two years after she was married. You may call it productivity, or merely a surprise!, she had a son 49 weeks later. Motherhood sprung in her emotions, love, and untiring dedication to juggle multiple responsibilities and duties. In her home of many languages, foods, cultures, traditions, and religious beliefs, she ran a tight ship. Flexibility, understanding, and love guided her in such environment and during her travels to meet the in-laws in Egypt.

Alma's relationship with her parents and the extended family in Puerto Rico helped shape her husband's interaction with them as a non-Spanish speaking new comer. The stories of that interaction are endless as are the stories of the many summers her children spent with Abuelo and Abuela.

Stories, memories, ambitions, dreams… the elements that shape ones character in this fast-paced world and a life's plan that is unknowingly laid out.

How Boring It Would Be!

On the top of a house porch
two wise black and white birds
surrounded by porch plants and trees
found the most peaceful place.
They stood in a tree branch looking at each other
and using together powerful strong sounds
saying, "We are not totally equal."
How boring it would be!

These two birds communicated the reason
for which diversity is always better.
Imagine my dear friend bird
if the Amazon, Nile and Hudson rivers were
surrounded with same trees, flowers and soil,
three rivers with the same direction and length
the same rocks, same fish and same width,
How boring it would be!

If people from the Asian countries
all had spoken the same indigenous language
producing men with the same size and face
women with unified body and eyes
wearing always the same dress style
praying to only one God or divinity
How boring it would be!

Imagine my brother bird
if you and I had the same colored feathers
eating the same seeds, sleeping in the same tree
How boring it would be!

United States, mono-lingual and mono-cultural
English killing Spanish, or perhaps Chinese
everyone's lunch of a ham and cheese sandwich,
not able to practice Christian, Hindu, or Muslim

going to school for only one purpose
marrying only their Anglo descendants,
children born with only one face
How boring it would be!

Europe, continuing to be an intolerant continent
misapprehension of navigators and explorers
with the persistency of only one God and religion.
Cultural conflicts, even misunderstanding
courteously not late for appointments
may even be considered overly prompt,
How boring it would be!

Touching the past and present of native Indians
different from one another in language and culture
Navajo, Pueblo, Apache, Inca, Aztec,
Maya, Taino, Carib, Esquimo.
Crafts, pottery, colors, *amuletos*
failure of Catholics and Protestants
imposing one language on the Indian,
How boring it would be!

We constantly pledge to the human being
To learn from us, the diversified birds
Always active, no sadness, no laziness
How boring it would be!

Chapter 8

DOORS OF OPPORTUNITY

My professorship journey in New York City had provided me with the privilege of encountering so many different cultures and different languages, and to look at the world from different perspectives and with an eye out for doors of opportunity. I had been blessed with students of all grade levels, and ethnic, cultural and linguistic backgrounds. Students from Puerto Rico, New York City and from all over the world have left deep footprints that are present in me, the educator, in the learner, and in the woman that I am. In this journey, I have taught both masters and doctoral students. I also taught, in my first years of teaching, a small group of undergraduate students.

The master's degree students did not stay long at the university, usually one to two years, but I worked closely with them throughout their college stay. Once they finished, they continued along with their lives. However, most of them, in one way or another way, expressed their gratitude for their learning experiences at the graduate college level. One of them, Gloria wrote me a meaningful note, saying:

"You killed me in your class, and I only received a B. However, today, I thank you for pushing me hard to be the best. I am not there yet, but I will be."

I was blessed to work with three types of graduate students. The first group was composed of those who came from abroad to do graduate study, usually a master's degree or a doctorate in language education programs. Most of these students came from Asian countries, although there were students from a diversity of foreign countries. They were labeled "foreign students," and they were usually in the United States for a relatively short period of time, usually with a student visa. The second group was composed of American citizens, mostly born in the mainland United States, who were mostly monolingual and proficient in English. The third group was composed of United States citizens who were born outside the United States but who had become American citizens, mostly through naturalization.

These three groups of students brought different learning styles and different attitudes and views about learning and teaching, which enhanced and broadened my views of the world and communities of opportunity.

The first group, the "foreign students," helped me to develop a sense of respect and admiration for cultural and linguistic diversity, as well as for looking at foreign students as significant academic contributors, both to the United States' educational system and their native countries. Although they would say that I had taught them, I feel that I learned from them more than they learned from me. In many ways, these foreign students reflected my own journey of opportunities in communities of resistance in the mainland United States. These students left family, living comfort, and language and embarked on an educational journey in a completely foreign and often hostile environment. They confronted professors who were not sensitive to their linguistic and cultural characteristics, and their learning styles. Furthermore, these students showed a lot of respect to everyone around them and assumed a determined attitude toward learning and toward life in general.

Throughout the years, I met foreign students from different parts of the world. Upon arrival to the United States and to the university, these students were tense, quiet, shy, and scared. The Asians bowed to you, the Latinos did not look in your eyes, and the Arabs spoke very slowly, looking in the distance. I always smiled at them, and I know my smile confused them since they did not know what it really meant. I spoke slowly, but not exaggeratedly slow, and I provided them with the main points of our conversation in writing, usually in an outline format. Then, I took them around the college; I showed them important offices, such as Admissions, the Registrar, the Library, the Bookstore, the International Students' Office, and the computer room. At the end of this first meeting, I invited them to come back within the same week, and I usually made the next appointment for them. When they came back, I identified them by their names and I asked:

"How are you doing?"

I allowed time for them to express themselves. Usually, due to the lack of direct experience with the English language or because they felt intimidated by the presence of "the professor," they did not say very much. I spent time with them, usually not talking about academic matters but about their countries, and their families. I also talked about myself: "I am from Puerto Rico." I showed it on a map. "I have been in this university for many years. I was very scare when I arrived in New York City."

We finished this second meeting by answering specific questions that they may have had. During the second meeting, foreign students felt a little bit more relaxed, and usually they had a list of questions about their program and courses. I again, gave them information in writing, for them to read at their leisure. I finished the second meeting by giving them a simple souvenir from the university: a folder, a pen, a flag, or a brochure. Then, I asked them to come back to my office within a week or two.

When the foreign students came back, they were at ease, smiling, and freely talking about "their new experience." From then on, they saw me as someone that they felt was on their side. When I saw them in the hall, I usually stopped, called them by their first or second name, depending on how it is done in their home country. After these friendly encounters, they usually stopped in my office with or without an appointment to say hello or to talk about their courses.

Usually, these students were closely attached to me, and they began to share their culture and their country with me. I made every possible effort to learn about their country and to share my knowledge with them. When they went to visit their countries, they usually brought me a souvenir that I displayed in the office, and often, they invited me to visit their countries, although, I usually did not accept their invitation while they were my students because I did not want to take advantage of their situation as students of mine. However, after graduation, I visited some of their counties and their homes.

The largest group of my foreign graduate students was Chinese. These Chinese graduate students came mainly from Taiwan and a few of them were from mainland China. These students were not usually affluent individuals but somehow they had a relative in United States or in their own country who took the financial responsibilities on paper so that the United States Embassy could approve the student visa. Once they were in the United States, many of them found different avenues to satisfy their financial needs. A significant number of these students had small part-time jobs within their communities.

Emily came from Taiwan with a student visa, completed her master's degree, worked as a teacher for four years with a working visa, and then returned to the university to engage in a doctoral program. She was my graduate assistant for several years. Emily possessed excellent technological skills that compensated for my lack of technological talent. One of the things that I remember about working with Emily was that although I tried to do several jobs at the same time, Emily kept me on track until I finished one job. After that, she reminded me about the next job. I felt much at ease with Emily, and she also confessed to me many times that she felt as if she was "with family" when she was with me. Sometimes I surprised myself by speaking in Spanish to Emily, and she would smile at me and say:

"No Spanish, Dr. C."

I usually did not touch my Asian students, since in addition to avoiding eye contact, they avoid touching. Puerto Ricans are very affectionate, and they tend to demonstrate it through touching and kissing. But before Emily returned to Taiwan, she hugged and kissed me. Working with Emily one day a week, taught me to be patient and to try to finish one job before starting the next one.

Japanese students came from the major cities of Tokyo and Osaka, although once in a while, I received one or two graduate students from a smaller city of Japan. The Japanese graduate students who came to my home institution were a mixed population in terms of age and financial means. One student, Toshiko was an educator in Japan, and one day she decided to come to a Jesuit university to pursue graduate work. Toshiko completed a master's degree and then continued toward a doctorate. In my office, I had a large picture that she had given to me, thanking me for guiding her and being her advisor in New York City. I never knew too much about her: she came here, bought an apartment, dressed well, and was very generous, although, she did not come from a rich family. She made financial arrangements to survive in Manhattan but never asked for advice or help. She shared with me her intellectual mind and the doors of opportunity that led her to an advanced college degree.

Another Japanese student who comes to my mind is Kay. She was the wife of a recognized Japanese businessman. She rebelled against the slavery treatment of her husband and divorced. When I met her, she had come to study for her doctorate, and she was working in a Japanese elementary bilingual school in Westchester. She had adopted many American attitudes and behaviors, although she felt as Japanese as Toshiko.

Throughout the years, I have kept up my friendship with these two Japanese women. They have taught me to be persistent, to have faith, and not to give up on dreams.

I have met two types of Korean students- the very young and the more mature. The young were usually financially stable, and came to study in the United States as a way of adding prestige to their academic background by studying and getting an American degree. The second group was composed of more mature students who often had saved money to earn a graduate degree to take back to Korea so that they could teach in a private/public school or university. Although they might have been in the United States alone, these students had very close ties with their families and they showed commitment to family well-being. There was one student who motivated me to study and visit Korea: Kyung Soon. She did all of her college work in the United States and came to my home university to pursue a doctoral degree. At the completion of the degree, we maintained a professional and social relationship, and our families became friends. Because we shared similar educational views, and she had the desire to experience college teaching, I facilitated her teaching experience as an adjunct professor. After she graduated, Kyung Soon invited me to visit Korea, and I accepted the invitation.

Kyung Soon's aunt Zook Choi, who is a professor in New Jersey was taking a group of colleagues to Korea. This, as well as an invitation by Youn Soo Hong, Kyung Soon's mother, provided me the opportunity to visit Korea and experience the rich cultural and historical background of this Asian country. Through lectures, visits to historical and cultural sites, as well as through interaction with Korean people, I learned that for many years, Korea served as a cultural, political, and economic support for China, Mongolia, and Japan. The Korean language was written around the same time that Europeans arrived in America. Although Korea was invaded by Japan, and its people were obligated to speak Japanese in public, including schools, the Korean language and culture never disappeared. Today, Seoul is one of the largest cities in the world, and South Korea has a very strong economy, which is likely due to its rigorous educational system.

After Kyung Soon completed her doctoral degree, we became close friends; she was constantly calling me for advice and guidance in professional and family matters. Today, we call each other two to three times per week. Throughout the years, I have become "Auntie Angela" to her, to her husband, and to her children. Her mother and I have a very good relationship, too, and we enjoy sharing social and family gatherings, as well as travel together. What I have learned from Kyung Soon and her family is that language and cultural differences do not impede communication and the sharing of higher values, attitudes, and affection.

The few African-Caribbean students, mainly from Jamaica, who came to study at my home institution, were mature individuals who had a tremendous desire to achieve a terminal degree in the field of education. Paying for tuition was a big challenge for them, and many of them worked in domestic jobs to finance part of their studies. Epsey was an educator from Jamaica who wanted to achieve a doctoral degree. She came to the United States while her husband stayed at their home in a small town in Jamaica. I found her Jamaican accent so beautiful and enriching.

Lucy and Rita are representatives of my South American students. Lucy is a Peruvian and a New York City kindergarten teacher who was a graduate student of mine at the university, though we never parted. We have kept in continuous personal contact: we talk almost every week, we visit each other, we go out and more importantly, we can talk about anything. When I have a "big success" or a "big problem" she is one of the first ones to know. Lucy has a highly spiritual sense that comforts me. She believes in the curative powers of the egg. When I need her, she brings an egg, and while I lay down, she rubs the egg all over my body for at least one hour. While doing so, we talk about everything- the family, the struggles, and the strategies we use to succeed. And by rubbing this egg, she can feel if I am angry, sick, or unhappy. I confide in her all of my struggles, my anxieties, or disillusions. She just listens to me. She provides me with confidence by saying:

"*Sí, con la ayuda de Dios todo se puede.*"(Yes, with God's help, everything is possible.)

I have known Rita, Lucy's sister, for more than 28 years. She is an educational administrator in the New York City Department of Education. I met Rita when she came to my office, carrying two small girls in a baby carrier, to find information about doctoral programs in education. She had completed a master's degree in education and wanted to find out about the possibility of pursuing a doctoral degree in education. She was a nanny to a well-known New York City politician and businessman. Someone had told her to make an appointment to talk to "Dr. C."

Looking at her face, I saw her hunger for knowledge and academic advancement, and I told her that I was going to push for her acceptance into the doctoral program. Her journey toward the completion of the program was difficult and slow; however she successfully made it to completion. At the end, she became part of my family. I was her wedding *madrina*. We talk to each other on a regular basis and get together for family reunions. I have visited Peru and her family and friends several times. Her father is my Papá, and her brother Angel, a priest in the isolated town of Concepción, is considered my *hermano*/brother.

I have had a long list of smart and distinguished American-born graduate students, who are different from the ones mentioned above. Usually, they were cut and dry; they were "all business," appreciative of what a professor did for them, but once the academic relationship ended, they moved on with their lives. But there were always exceptions. Two names come to my mind: Ruth and Diane. Ruth is a New York City language educator who came to me in search of an additional teaching certificate. But since the beginning, I found myself professionally attracted to this teacher who was interested in expanding her learning and teaching skills. She received her certificate and continued toward her doctorate. We had many conversations on how to help Latino children succeed and the many obstacles and challenges their parents face. Today, we are good friends, and I consider her a closer colleague- closer than most of my full-time university peers. She was a regular adjunct in my teaching program. We have written together, and we respect each other very much.

Diane, a US-born American who studied Spanish in school, became a high school Spanish teacher and married a Puerto Rican man. Diane is an excellent teacher- very committed to her students and to the Spanish language. She is very proud of teaching Spanish, and wrote her dissertation on her Spanish students. She retired from her high school job and is now teaching at the college level. She taught me to express my joy of teaching and to publicly disseminate my philosophy of the positive role of bilingual education.

Several decades ago, my home institution was blessed by a group of Puerto Rican professionals, mostly college professors and school administrators, who enrolled in a doctoral program. Most of these individuals received financial support from their Puerto Rican institution to engage in a doctoral program in New York City. Professors from New York City went to Puerto Rico during the academic year, usually on the weekends, and the graduate students came to New York City during the summers. This group of students was highly motivated and highly competent. Half of them were not entirely proficient in English; however they had the knowledge, skills, and disposition to work hard toward their degrees. I had the opportunity to be the bridge between the Puerto Rican graduate students and my colleagues. I was directly involved in this project, and I felt very proud of my *paisanos*.

In teaching these Puerto Rican graduate students, American professors, usually Anglos experienced a culture shock which changed their mind and attitudes. My colleagues were shocked by the caliber of these graduate students, and even more so by their hospitality. These graduate students took professors to their homes, showed them the island of Puerto Rico, prepared special dinners, and gave them generous gifts. And, at the same time, they were humble and hard-working individuals. Some of my colleagues confused lack of English proficiency with lack of knowledge. For example, one dynamic and competent doctoral student had a hard time in an ethnography course because the professor corrected the grammar more than the content of his research project. Another doctoral student, who was a competent supervisor who worked in the Puerto Rico Department of Education, had serious difficulties writing a project on the different reading methods implemented in Puerto Rican public schools. Since English was not her first language, and she made several English grammar mistakes writing the project, she had many difficulties getting the professor's approval of the project. The professor graded her mainly on the grammatical errors and not on the content of the work. But, in spite of all these challenges, almost every member of the two participating cohorts finished the program and graduated.

Another Puerto Rican student of mine although not from the cohort, is Diane. She came to New York City to pursue a master's degree. She taught in a New York City high school for about five years. Her special education students, especially Latinos, adored her, in spite of her being a very strict teacher. She moved to college teaching, taught two years in a New York City college, then the warmer climate of Florida enticed her to move to a southern university. In Florida, she experienced "academic politics," where the administration of the college asked her to treat the "donor students" better than the "non-donors." Diana, a woman of ethical professional roots, decided not to stay in that climate. Today, she is a recognized professor in North Carolina. We are in constant communication. One aspect of Diane that I admire is her continuous effort to be objective in a subjective academic world. From her, I have learned to continue the struggle, even in communities of resistance.

The third group of students is made of what I call "mainstream students," who are American individuals who were born outside of the United States, but became part of the American mainstream through naturalization. Two individuals come to my mind: Vivian and Veronica. Vivian is a smart Cuban woman whose parents immigrated to the United States after Fidel Castro took power in Cuba. Vivian struggled to survive in the United States. Her journey took her to Spain, then to Miami, and then to New Jersey. She became a bilingual teacher and one day, because she was recommended by someone, she visited my office. For four years, we worked together on her dissertation project. One night, at about 8 PM, Vivian came to my Lincoln Center office. Her face showed frustration and lack of sleep (that is the way it goes with a dissertation). She said:

"I am ready to put this document in the garbage."

I looked in her eyes and said:

"Vivian, there is a garbage can in this room, and, at the end of this conversation, you can put your dissertation right there."

I started to explain to Vivian what needed to be revised (we had done several revisions before). At the end of the conversation, she said, "good night" and left. Of course, she did not put the dissertation in the garbage, and she graduated that year. After that, she became a school principal in a very high socio-economic neighborhood. After two years, she realized that the student body of the school was not the population she wanted to work with. She left this comfortable position for a deputy superintendent job in a diverse school district in southern New Jersey. We wrote a book together, *Language Minority Students in the Mainstream Classroom*, which became a popular textbook in many universities. Vivian has been an inspiration of growth. She is a constant learner and a facilitator of learning. From her, I have learned to not stop until the ideal academic setting is found.

Veronica came to the United States from Costa Rica when she was a little girl. Although her first language is English, she has been able to learn and use the Spanish language. She raised two children alone. For many years, she struggled in New York City, and then moved to a small town in Georgia, thinking that, financially, she was going to do better. However, she did not find academic and social satisfaction in this small town, and she made the decision to come back to New York City and move on with her life. She enrolled in a doctoral education program in my home university, and I guided her through the difficult journey of writing a dissertation. It took her a long time because she confronted illness at the end of the program, but she never lost sight of her goal of becoming a doctor of education. She did graduate. She is a super star staff developer for the New York City educational system. What I have learned from her is not to give up the dreams of professional development and teacher betterment, but to aspire, and to work hard for what is wanted in life.

There are many more stories that I can add in this chapter, but do to a lack of space, I am not allowed to include them. However, I want to acknowledge the influence of the following former students: Ana, Aramina, Lillybeth, Christina, Edward (Eddie), Felix, Doña Panchín, Jane, Julia, Judy, Lourdes, Lucía, Lydia, Magali, Manuel, Martin, Mayra, María, Mary, Milagros (Wanda), Mirqueya, Nitza, Olga, Rosamaría, Victor, and Yiyi.

Thinking about my former students' educational experiences and attributes provides me with a sense of satisfaction with my teaching journey. And I think:

"God, help me to continue motivating my students so that I have more Debbies, Kyung Soons, Dianes, and Veronicas!"

Advocate for New York City Students and Families

Magali Figueroa-Sánchez

Professor Magali Figueroa-Sánchez has been advocating for New York City students and families for the past thirty-two years. When she entered school as a child in the South Bronx, there were no bilingual programs. She acquired English through schooling, in both Catholic and public schools, where she faced many hardships because of her lack of prior exposure to English. She struggled and succeeded, graduating from Cardinal Spellman High School with the Gold Medal in Spanish.

The memories of those school years motivated her to enter the teaching field. She learned of the Bilingual Pupil Services (BPS) program from her mother, who was an educator at PS 60 in the South Bronx. BPS was a program in the New York City public school system designed to prepare bilingual teachers through a combination of intensive internship experiences over several years in bilingual classrooms and tuition support for college coursework in bilingual education. At Lehman College, she completed her baccalaureate degree, 'cum laude' with a major in Puerto Rican Studies and a minor in Bilingual Education. She continued and received her Master's of Science in Education with specialization in Early Childhood. After years of working in different leadership roles, Professor. Figueroa-Sánchez entered Hunter College and received an Advanced Certificate in Administration and Supervision of Schools.

Professor Figueroa-Sánchez was awarded the Lehman Urban Teacher Education certificate in recognition of her work in New York City schools. Dr. Figueroa-Sánchez wrote her first article, "Building Emotional Literacy: Groundwork to Early Learning" which was published in the ACEI in the summer of 2008.

In 1999, Figueroa-Sánchez applied and was appointed to a leadership position in which she supported pre-service and in-service teachers in education, as well as faculty. Her work as Project Support Coordinator for Lehman's Paraprofessional Development program resulted in many of the paraprofessionals attaining their Bachelor's as well as their Master's degrees in education. As an ardent advocate for students preparing to become bilingual teachers, she saw her role as a mentor to teacher candidates in helping them balance family, school, and their personal relationships. She was inspired to work on her doctorate while coordinating three federally-funded grant programs at Lehman College.

Upon completion of her doctorate at Fordham University, she took a position as an assistant professor in education at Eugenio María de Hostos Community College of the City University of New York in the South Bronx, with the purpose of advocating for bilingualism and mentoring immigrant students. She sees her advocacy work as a natural outgrowth of the experiences she had through observing her family's work, her professional preparation, and the professional roles that she assumed over her career as an advocate for community and professional organizations supporting the advancement of minority groups.

Presently, Professor Figueroa-Sánchez is the Executive Director of the Hostos Children's Center, Inc., which serves the student parents of the campus at Eugenio María de Hostos Community College. This center supports student parents to secure an educational, safe, and caring environment for their young children while they complete their course work to attain their college degrees.

Harding Park

Masaaki Takahashi

From Manhattan raining
Up along the Hudson River smoggy and misty
Drive to Harding Park, a Puerto-Rican dreaming place
Saw fishing men on the River bank
Goose horses swimming their tails over the River surface
Hear early summer birds singing their songs among bushes and trees there
Suddenly appeared blocks of tall buildings of the Town
Across over between gray sky and misty river
Tell me the names of them
Then a child near by answered
The tallest one of the left is Alexis, his name
And the right side blocks Kartskil
Reminds me of soul of tales, old Rip Van Winkle.

Chapter 9

PUERTO RICO IN THE BRONX

Several years passed; my three children went to elementary, then secondary school. They all finished college and had moved out to their own apartments. Barney was a police officer and had married. Olveen was at Harvard School of Social Policy to expand his medical career and Angeles Ivette was already attending medical school at New York University. The three of them moved out and were involved in their own personal, professional and academic lives. My husband and I had received tenure and promotions in our universities and were moving along with our professional and personal lives. I continued teaching and working on the many tasks of the professorship. Christmas passed and I was preparing my spring courses. The telephone rang and it was one of my former students.

"This is Debbie, reminding you that I have sent you an invitation to come to Belize," Deborah said. "I am hoping that you can come to Belize and spend two weeks with a group of Belizean professors. We are in the process of developing a Language and Literacy Center, and we would love your guidance and advice in this process."

Deborah had finished her master's degree in Teaching English as a Second Language and was working as a professor at the University of Belize. She was charged with the responsibility of creating a Center for Language and Literacy. While in New York, Debbie had shown strong leadership skills, as well as a deep knowledge of the teaching and learning of English as a Second Language. And, although Belize is an English-speaking country, its language is unique due to the many linguistic and ethnic influences of its people and surroundings.

"Yes, Debbie, I am now ready to visit your country and get first hand experience on the teaching and learning of a second language in Belize," I said.

This invitation provided me the opportunity to continue to think about my students and the doors of opportunity that they had opened for themselves and to me. I had taught in Puerto Rico and in New York City in a variety of educational environments. I had met a diversity of students. I had taught the young, the adolescent, the adult, the Asian, the Latino, the African American, the Caribbean, the European, and the United States native English-speaking student. And, now, most of these students were in leadership positions and wanted to keep the professional relationship with their former teacher.

I went to Belize, and I spent two weeks with humble and intelligent professors and administrators at the University of Belize to assist in the planning of the language center. The Belize experience provided me with the knowledge and exchange of ideas on how to teach "standard" English to individuals who live in an English-speaking country, but who are surrounded by culturally and linguistically mixed communities. Most of the people that I had the opportunity to interact with in Belize were knowledgeable and successful in what they did, in part due to their rich hopes and sensitivity to the important role that language plays in learning and teaching.

After returning from Belize, I went back to my routine as a professor: teaching, meetings, research, and scholarly writing. The academic life continued to be as busy as always. I was completing two manuscripts, one on *Teaching English as a Second Language*, another one on *Parents and Schools*. The latter one was co-authored by a brilliant colleague, Clement London, who was an expert in community matters, social sciences, and curriculum. I also continued to speak on the topic of best educational practices for students for whom English is not their native language.

One day, I was at Columbia University speaking to a group of teachers, and, at lunchtime, Lucy, a teacher from the Bronx, sat next to me and asked me where I was living. When I mentioned that I was living in the southeast part of the Bronx, in the Soundview area, she told me that she owned a house in an interesting community nearby called Harding Park. I told her that I had never heard of the name Harding Park before.

"By the way, there is a house with a waterfront for sale for a very good price," she said.

"A waterfront house in the Bronx?" I asked.

Because I showed interest in the house, she promised to take me to see it. And of course, I was expecting to see a house, not a bungalow, which might even have been better described as a shack. I saw dilapidated remains of a bungalow that had seen better days. However, the location was an interesting one, with views of Hunts Point and Manhattan. I did not say anything to Lucy because I did not want to hurt her good will of showing me the house. And, I did not say anything to my family at home, either.

Two nights later, I drove alone to Harding Park to see how the property looked during the night. I saw the view of the lighted Manhattan skyline reflected in the water, moved by cool ocean winds. I saw the lights of the Triborough Bridge, now the Robert F. Kennedy, as well as the George Washington Bridge. What a spectacular view! Suddenly, I became interested in this tiny piece of land, not for the purpose of making it my residence, but as a small vacation place, perhaps with a trailer or even a new bungalow, to just go there and admire the lights of Manhattan, and be refreshed by the crisp air coming up from the water. I told my husband of the Harding Park house I went to see. I did not say anything about its condition.

"It has a beautiful view. You have to see it. We will go there one of these nights. I want you to see it," I said.

He did not say anything; he was comfortable living in the two-family house that we owned, and he had no intention to move. He liked that the two-family house provided an additional income.

Three days later, I took my husband, at nighttime, to see the house from the outside. When I signaled the house to him, he asked me:

"Are you telling me that you are talking about that shack?"

"Yes, but look at the view," I said.

And immediately, he said:

"No, I am not paying money for just a view. Oh, no! We, you and me, are not buying this. Please forget that we came here."

I kept quiet; I entered the car and only said, "Well, I like it very, very much!"

The entire following week, I kept insisting on the merits of buying this tiny property. I bombarded my husband with the idea.

"We should not discard the idea of buying this property. We can get a vacation trailer and put it there."

But my husband knew that once I wanted to get something, I would not stop until I got it, even if I had to make many sacrifices. Two months later, he agreed to give me the pleasure of having this property. He was still not too convinced, but we bought it anyway.

It did not take him long to become interested in the place. He liked the view, the fresh air, the country look, and the simplicity of the place. We agreed to build our residence on our new property and move to Harding Park. We immediately started the process of building a new house, without destroying the existing house front, so that it looked more like a renovation. My husband decided to build it himself. After the foundation of the house was built, we were fortunate to buy another tiny piece of land next to the property to use it as a small backyard and patio.

I give a lot of credit to my husband because although he had some experience in concrete house improvement and renovation in Puerto Rico, he had no knowledge of how to build a wooden house in the United States, especially considering the hot and cold weather of a temperate climate. He observed other constructions, he asked questions, and he practiced in our new house as he built it.

Harding Park, a neighborhood that until a few years ago was not even on the map of the Bronx, is a peninsula, surrounded by the waters of the Bronx River, the East River, and the Long Island Sound. In the north, there is the community of Clason Point, and not far toward the northeast, is the Soundview area with its yet undiscovered Soundview Park. From Harding Park, there is a view of Hunts Point Terminal Market, the island of Manhattan and the RFK Bridge, the 59th Street Bridge, the Washington Bridge, the Empire State Building, and the Chrysler building. To the east, there is La Guardia Airport, Rikers Island, and the prestigious community of Whitestone in Queens. Because of its size, all the above places can be seen from almost every place in Harding Park. There is a combination of old trees and new ones, narrow roads and dirt roads, vacant lots, and relatively small pieces of abandoned city land near the water.

The land of Harding Park has changed hands several times over the decades. In 1898, Thomas Highs obtained the rights to 100 acres of land, and, in 1924, the heirs of Leland Tompkins took control, naming the land Harding Park after the late president Warren G. Harding. Tiny parcels were rented to people to build their summer bungalows. The families who, by then, had built and winterized their bungalows, paid ground rent to remain.

In 1978, the city took control of this land after Federal Homes, the last private owners of Harding Park, defaulted on its taxes. The city, its new tenants and Mr. Mena, (one of the first Puerto Rican leaders of Harding Park), chief among them, negotiated for two years on how to repair the streets and sewers and turn the land over to the tenants, who were paying about $25 a month. But when negotiations broke down and tenants started a rent strike, the city threatened eviction. This provoked a new round of meetings and letter writing and a lawsuit, which was eventually dropped.

In 1982, after three years of negotiation, the deed was turned over to the residents through their Homeowners Association for an average of $3,000 for each lot. The Association paid $390,000 and made the difference with mortgages. Most of the residents became owners for the first time. It was the leadership of the few Puerto Ricans who had move to Harding Park that pressured the mayor of New York City to negotiate with the community members.

In this community, there is a significant number of Puerto Ricans, many of them of first generation, which is in contrast to the original people: Irish and German descendents, most of whom have left the neighborhood. Many Puerto Ricans, who were renting in nearby apartments, heard the news that for only $2000 or $3000 they could become homeowners. So, they searched for bungalows for sale. And when a German or Irish put their bungalows up for sale, the Puerto Ricans were the first ones to buy. Names like Rodríguez, Rivera, and Pérez became Harding Park homeowners. This first generation of Puerto Ricans was attracted to this neighborhood by the beauty of the area, by the idea of renovating the bungalows and having their first house, and by the reasonable prices of the properties.

Many residents and many neighbors call Harding Park, "Little Puerto Rico," because many of the renovated bungalows have similarities to the humble houses of the *barriadas* of Puerto Rico. Like residents of Puerto Rico, the families surround their property with fences made of cement and painted iron; the balconies look likes many of the balconies in the Puerto Rico *barriadas*; and even some of the styles of the houses are similar to those built in Puerto Rico in the 1940s and 1950s. The houses are fenced using cement or cycled fence materials. In Puerto Rico, owners built fences to protect their property from neighbors that might want to expand their property land at the expense of unfenced houses. Harding Park owners have a preference for very bright colors for their balconies or fences, similar to Puerto Ricans in Puerto Rico. Some of the houses have similar structural construction as those found in Puerto Rico: little balconies, cement foundation, and Caribbean model entrances.

Like many poor residents of the *barriadas* in Puerto Rico, the story of the first Puerto Rican residents of Harding Park is one of persistence, ingenuity, and risk. Their voyage has not been easy, and residents have been persistent in their efforts to stay in Harding Park.

When we first moved to Harding Park, there were few paved roads, sidewalks, streets, or street lamps. The houses did not have 'certificates of occupancies' given by the New York City Building Department indicating safety living conditions. Cracked clay pipes pumped sewage into the river. Every resident struggled to repair and to provide maintenance to their own property against the indifference of many other residents, politicians, and government agencies. And to promote the rebuilding of Harding Park, Mayor Edward Koch took an unusual step: he exempted shacks from building codes.

Harding Park became a community of about 240 homeowners, the houses of which were mostly badly constructed bungalows, largely made up of boxes, cheap old wood, and recycled roof shingles. As in Amish barn raisings, only with a salsa undertone, the Solises helped the Perezes, who helped the Rodriguezes who helped the Lopezes. As the 1980s rolled into the 1990s and 2000s, summer gardens multiplied and bloomed, and houses were upgraded and rose to two floors. These residents gave up visits to parents and grandparents in Puerto Rico and pocketed the money for cement and building materials. Housewives became auxiliary carpenters to their husbands, picking up pointers on shingling a roof or insulating a wall; husbands learned how to install boilers, and to route electrical wires. It took them years to rebuild, and many of them are still pounding out new sections.

At that time, Harding Park was a natural beauty surrounded by garbage, shacks, abandoned houses, stray dogs and cats, chickens, rabbits, ducks, and every other imaginable domestic animal. Urban city rules and regulations were seldom followed. But with the arrival of new residents, specifically Puerto Rican professionals, the neighborhood changed and became cleaner. There are a large number of renovated houses, and there are no longer stray dogs and cats. However, still today, there are hens and roosters in the small roads of the community. Wild rabbits run through the neighborhood, coming from nearby Soundview Park. In spite of, or perhaps due to, this lack of planning and development, Harding Park remains one of the most beautiful pieces of land in the Bronx, and perhaps in the whole city of New York.

Still today, homeowners are guided by a not-for- profit organization, the Harding Park Homeowners Association. The Association is required to collect monthly fees to repair streets, maintain the water mains, and to pay insurance and real estate taxes on the vacant lots and driveways. But residents, who pay property taxes, still have to clear their own snow, fix their own streetlights, and keep up vacant lots. The city picks up the garbage and responds to major emergencies.

At the beginning, Harding Park was a community of low socio-economic white residents. Today, homeowners include middle class retired families, as well as a small group of young families, (mainly the retired families' children and their grandchildren). There is also a small group of professionals who are buying and renovating the houses in the area. Even David Valentín, the renowned violinist lives in Harding Park, and loves the country style and simplicity of the community that is within minutes of the crowded urban areas.

When Puerto Ricans began to move in, the old residents were afraid that this new ethnic group could put them out of their residences, loosing the land that they had aggressively conquered. On the other hand, Puerto Ricans were afraid of the white residents. They were afraid of confronting them, that they might take reprisal against those who were acquiring properties. And at the beginning, there were several confrontations between the two groups- some houses were burned, cars were vandalized.

During my first three years in Harding Park, the old white residents showed me that I was not welcomed in the neighborhood. Every time that I planted an evergreen in front of my house, it was destroyed during the night. But, the next day, when I discovered the absence of the evergreen, I went to the plant shop and bought and planted another one. It went like that for some time, until the old and the new residents began to become acquainted with each other and realize that Harding Park was for everyone, and that no one ethnic group was trying to eliminate the other group.

Throughout the years, there is an understanding that this piece of land is the land of all those individuals who want to live and protect the community, including all nationalities and races. Puerto Ricans who live in this neighborhood are obliged to feel proud because this Little Puerto Rico has managed to impart a sense of Puerto Rican pride. It is not a sophisticated neighborhood, but somehow, it has the physical appearance of the houses built in Puerto Rico in the 1960s, 1970s and 1980s.

I lived almost twenty years in this beautiful and unnoticed area. I wrote many pages of my scholarly work while looking at the bay formed by the Bronx River, the East River, and the beginning of the Long Island Sound. I truly think that Harding Park is an unknown little paradise. The hungry real estate developers have not yet discovered this Caribbean jewel.

In Search of Knowledge: A Journey of Reflection, Collaboration and Transformation

Aida A. Nevárez-La Torre,

At a very young age, Dr. Aida A. Nevárez-La Torre knew she wanted to be a teacher. Her maternal grandfather, great uncle, and mother had all paved the way for her by being "maestros" of children and youth in rural sectors of Puerto Rico. Soon after getting married, her parents left the mountains of Puerto Rico in search of a better life in the metropolitan areas of San Juan and Guaynabo. There she witnessed how her parents' struggled to improve the quality of their life by working two or three jobs at a time and going to school, while raising three daughters. According to them, education was necessary to build a better future and accomplish any goals in life. Her father held conservative values, but with a feminist outlook. When he was growing up, family responsibilities prevented him from attending school, but for his daughters, he wanted something better. He used to say, "I do not want my daughters to depend on any man when they grow up; they should be professionals, ready to face the world on their own terms." This admonition always guided Nevárez-La Torre's search for knowledge.

As a child she became a voracious reader of different genres, everything from comic books, Charles Dickens, and Edgar Allen Poe to Los Cuentos de Juan Bobo, Eugenio Mariá de Hostos, and Sor Juana Ineś de la Cruz. Her interest in language education emerged from her own experiences as an English language learner, in a private all- English school on the island. She later became fully bilingual in Spanish and English while completing graduate studies in the United States. Issues of the politics of language and identity were always in the forefront as she negotiated being a teacher of English on the island and teaching bilingual education in the States. As a teacher in the US, she has always boldly confronted forces that attempt to silence the mind, and spirits of those who speak languages other than English.

While studying for her doctorate at Harvard Graduate School of Education, she advocated for the language rights of multilingual students through her participation as an editor of the Harvard Educational Review and as an organizer in the English Plus Movement in Boston, MA. Educated under a tradition that stressed teacher involvement in the community, she created partnerships between universities and community organizations and directed family centers in schools to better serve the educational and social needs of multilingual families in Harrisburg and Philadelphia, PA.

As principal investigator, she has directed grants from prestigious organizations like the Spencer Foundation, the US Department of Education, and the Fells Foundation. She was awarded fellowships to study and conduct research from the Lindback Foundation, Lily Endowment, and Christian College Coalition.

At present, she is the director of the Office of Multilingual Education at Fordham University in New York City. She also is the Senior Editor of the *Journal of Multilingual Education Research*. Her scholarly writings examine alternative ways to educate practitioners, which incorporate reflection, collaboration, and transformation on issues of language education. She uses a critical lens to expose oppressive dimensions of education that limit the talents and creativity of educators who work with multilingual students. She carries this message in the book entitled: *The Power of Learning from Inquiry: Teacher Research as a Professional Tool in Multilingual Settings* (IAP Publishers). The educational opportunities of migrant workers and their families is the focus of her latest investigation.

It is clear that her quest for learning and advocating for the educational rights of multilingual students will persist as she continues to work with and inspire new generations of educators.

Single Women

We are single, yes, we are
we are not married by our own choice
we have children, we have none
we are happy with the way we are.

We push and push to get to the top
we are certain to get what we really want
we work many hours on a seven day week
we fight many battles for little recognition.

We have a life full of joy and satisfaction
we are determined to carry the plan
we are not worried about the difficulties
we know difficulties will always exist.

We think that life is always challenging
we see challenges wherever we go
we try to live one day at a time
we, surrounded by dreams and hopes.

We are pre-programmed to do what men usually do
We- not men- but we, are the real strong ones
we do carpentry, put to work the heating system
we repair the faucet and do uncomplicated electricity.

We work in the garden and cut the grass
we take care of the house utilities
we go for groceries and also cook them
we manage to cope with every detail.

We wash the car, not afraid of changing tires
we get gas from the pump, and check the oil
we travel long distances to get what we want
we always put fire in whatever we do.

We have learned to deal with greedy businessmen
we screen the real face of the religious leaders
we read the mind of the powerful bosses
we look at their smiles toned at a "single woman."

We are the single women of the world
we are vigilant and ready to move
we are always ready to enjoy our life
we, a life of accomplishments and many to come.

Chapter 10

CLOSING AND OPENING CIRCLES

One early evening in February, I came back to my office from teaching one of my favorite courses, 'Second Language Acquisition.' The evening was closing in; the sun had finally slipped behind the closest mountains to New York City; it could no longer be seen. So, I knew that it was time to head home. Typically, I would have called my husband to let him know that I was on my way, but that night, I wanted to surprise him by getting home earlier than usual. I turned off the office computer. I put on all my winter accessories: the coat, the scarf, the hat, and the gloves. I walked to the garage to pick up my car. The friendly people at the garage had my car already lined up to go.

I drove north up the West Side Highway, which at that hour was bumper-to-bumper traffic. I always loved to take this highway and admire the reflections of the New Jersey lights on the Hudson River. The Cross Bronx Expressway was something else; surrounded by dangerous trucks and all types of foreign and domestic cars, all in a hurry, speeding and changing lanes as frequently as possible. I overcame all the driving obstacles and I finally took the White Plains Road exit and headed to Harding Park, my neighborhood.

I was in front of my house and I noticed stillness and silence, but I was not surprised because my neighborhood was always quiet at this time of the night. And it should have been that way because it was February, when it gets dark early, and the trees and gardens wait for the authoritative presence of the wise bug to tell everyone how close or how far spring really is.

"The house at least should be lighted; my husband is inside waiting for me," I thought.

I turned off the car's engine, and I locked the doors. I closed the garage door and walked through the frozen sleepy grass toward the back entrance of my house. I put the key in the lock and opened the door. No radio on, no TV on, no lights on. I turned on the lights, I looked around, but I did not see anyone. I went up to the second floor where the bedrooms are. I checked my bedroom and I did not see anyone there. I went to the next bedroom, and there was no one there, either. I went back down to the kitchen, and I noticed that the stove was as cold as a dead body, and there was no cooked food. I went up to the third bedroom and I noticed that there was a dresser missing. I went back to my bedroom, checked the drawers of the chest, and there, I noticed that my husband's clothes were missing, as well as other personal items of his. Although there was no written message, I began to wonder if my husband had left the house and me.

I sat down. I knew that the relationship between my husband and me was not good, but I never realized that it was going to turn this way. I always thought that my marriage could be fixed and saved.

"Do not panic. Do not call anyone. Tonight, you only think about the steps to take in the next two to three days," I said to myself.

"What is next?" I asked. I had no answer to this question.

No one is really prepared for what life brings the next day. And that night, I realized that after 33 years of living with my husband, my marriage was probably ending. Awakening to this reality was shocking. I thought that I was not prepared for divorce; I had never thought about the possibility of being alone in a big house, with no children and no husband. That night, the house seemed bigger than it really was. I suddenly became afraid of being alone in the house. What if the heating system stops? What if there is a problem with the electricity or the running water? I felt totally incompetent to deal with these issues. I just sat in a small rocking chair and allowed my mind to review what was happening.

In the past, specifically, ten years ago, my husband and I used to do everything together. We took trips together, we went to social activities together, we took the grandchildren to the park together, we went to church together, and we attended professional activities together. The professional activities were usually invitations to me that I expanded to include my husband. And he gladly went with me, and I was proud to have him next to me.

But for some unclear reason to me, my husband began to feel uncomfortable near me. Our intimate life deteriorated, and he began to distance himself from me. During the last five years, he had refused to accompany me to conferences and professional activities. Then, he refused to entertain with me or go to social activities with me. "*Vete tú que yo no voy*" (Go, I am not going.); he usually told me when an invitation came. And I observed that he was in a state of deep reflection that he did not want to share with me.

I thought that he had a professional ego problem or that he was deeply depressed; for I was an active professor, and he was completely inactive in his profession. He had no academic involvement, and he felt uncomfortable and out of touch in professional settings. In addition, I was in the vibrant and active field of bilingual education and teaching English as a Second Language, and he was in the field of teaching remedial mathematics to undergraduate students. He had no motivation to share his academic experiences. On the contrary, I had a high level of motivation driving me to get involved in my profession. I thought that he began to see my professional career as his greatest enemy. And, to some extent, I felt sorry for him; he was frustrated by being near a highly involved college professor.

My husband spent a lot of time inside the house, looking at four empty walls. His job required him to be on campus only two days a week for only three or four hours, mainly in the mornings. And, different from me, he did not get involved in the professional work of conducting research, writing scholarly publications, and attending professional meetings and conferences. He was just stuck to teaching undergraduate college students how to add, subtract, and do simple algebraic problems. He attended one or two department meetings every month. Our professional roles were completely different and unbalanced, keeping us emotionally and professionally apart.

I was the opposite of him. I spent time outside of the house taking care of my professional, civic, and community responsibilities. I used to have three to four professional meetings a day and I had to be on the university campus four days a week, mainly during the evenings. Most of my students were teachers who took classes at the end of their working day. These teachers came to the university to polish their academic skills or to complete a required degree to get a permanent teaching job. In other words, I had to stay at work usually until seven or eight o'clock at night. My husband was not able to understand the reasons why I had to stay at my job until the early hours of the night.

And this home/time discrepancy created a level of distance between the two of us. We grew apart; we did not talk as much as we used to. Even when I came home with a wonderful piece of professional news such as the publication of a new article or getting a new consultancy, my husband was not enthusiastic or interested in knowing about it. There were several pieces of writing that I wrote and I added his name, just to motivate him to stay involved with the professional academic world. He never read or talked about these publications.

"I want you to read this article that I published in this journal," I said.

"*Ponlo por ahí*" (Put it any place.), he replied, but he would never read it.

He complained to friends and family, but not to me. I did not see his loneliness, although I had noticed some resentment in my husband's infrequent communication to me. I blamed his indifference on depression caused by his serious problems with his job. I kept saying to myself that everything was fine, although I noticed the distance between us growing. My husband became even more silent, and I tried to intervene to get him medical help but he did not welcome my intervention. This tenuous relationship went on like this for almost three years. It became even more serious during the last year when he was asked to leave his job, a job that seemed to be the only motivation and joy he had.

I kept asking myself what had happened to this man. My husband and I raised three excellent children in a house full of love. I remember that at the beginning, we had to make many sacrifices and choices to raise and educate three small children, but in the end, we became successful parents. He and I were on top of everything: homework, health, friends, school, clothing, food, entertainment, and good manners. But my husband had no social networks and no friends; he was totally isolated; and relied completely on the company of his siblings. Playing dominos with them became his main form of entertainment.

The night that my husband left, I called my son Barney, who informed me that his father had moved to a small apartment that we had in a two-family house. After ending the conversation with my son, I decided that my first move would be to try to convince my husband to sit in front of me, and talk to me about the issues that made him leave. I wanted to bring him back home. Three days later, I went to see him at the apartment where he had settled. I knocked at the door; he opened the door of the apartment but did not invite me to go inside. And with the door half opened, I said:

"I want you to tell me why you left me. I deserve to be told. I am not asking you to come back, but do not leave me without giving me an explanation," I said.

"I have nothing to say to you," he said. I looked at him and then left his apartment.

I realized that our intimate relationship was finished, and that I had to continue with my life. Marriage is a solid relationship grounded in love, trust, and sentiment; when that intimate circle broke, I found myself alone and fighting a bitter battle over trust, children's confidence, property, and money. Eight months later, we divorced.

My professional life continued. At that time, my colleagues had voted and elected me chair of one of the departments in the school. The intensive involvement required of this new position was helpful in erasing the sad experiences of a divorce.

As chair of the Department of Curriculum and Teaching, I was in charge of 27 faculty members. At the beginning, I faced resistance from a group of my fellow professors. I was shocked to know that those that were considered to be, not only my colleagues, but my "friends" did not give me initial support. One of those colleague friends went to the department chair meetings that I chaired and deliberately read doctoral dissertations and admission materials during the meeting, without giving attention to the business of the meeting. His attitude made me sad, but I did not say anything. Others contradicted me on a regular basis.

"I respect your point of view. Perhaps you may want to provide additional information and make a presentation at the next meeting," I responded.

Most of the time, the faculty member would forget the invitation, and business would continue as usual. But after several months, the faculty got to know my administrative style and tended to argue less, although I could not get them to be more productive or creative. My strategy was to prepare myself very well and not to argue with them in front of the rest of the faculty. I spent many hours in the office, updating office files, activating students' information, and drafting informational documents. I often worked on Saturdays and Sundays.

Fortunately, I had a competent and loyal secretary. Twelve years before becoming chair, I met Lissette, a Dominican woman who came to the University looking for a job as a secretary. A colleague and I were in need of a secretary for a funded program, and Lissette was hired for this position. I worked with her on a daily basis, and although I demanded a lot from her, she always delivered. We became a good team and better friends. When I became chair of the department, I took her with me as an administrative secretary. When I had a difficult task to do, she always came to the rescue. On paper, I looked more academically capable than her, but no one has the vision and wisdom of this woman. I trusted her so much, and still do! She was always there for me. If I needed to get a document or an address or anything else, I had assurance in my first call to Lissette. And she never said "no" to me. This young woman was my closest academic confident.

The days seemed to grow longer; more hours of direct sun; and tears were constantly filling my eyes. Life shifting as life does. It was the beginning of spring. Buildings seemed sleepy still, but the streets in Manhattan were crowded still. I was in the daily routine of being a department chair, a professor, lecturing, reading papers, and attending meetings. After one of these chair meetings I had the need to go outside of the building and have a cup of coffee, even if it was *un café ralo* (weak coffee).

I went to a small coffee shop near the university. Next to me, I overheard a man in a blue suit speaking in Spanish to one of his clients on his cell phone. When he was finished with his call, I asked,

"Hi, are you from Puerto Rico?"

"Yes, I am from Bayamón," he said.

And, not out of the ordinary, I engaged in an informal conversation with this stranger about why Puerto Ricans move to the mainland United States.

"I left Puerto Rico for educational reasons, and I am always in a constant state of nostalgia," I said.

"Me, too. ¡*Extraño a mi Puerto Rico*! (I am home sick!) I love to listen to songs such as *En mi Viejo San Juan, Lamento Borincano* and *Verde Luz*," he said. "These songs give me strength while I am out of Puerto Rico; my Puerto Rican identity goes with me everywhere I go," he said.

I added:

" No matter what people in the mainland United States or on the island of Puerto Rico think or say, even if Puerto Ricans were born in Chicago, Boston, Orlando or New York City, even if they are of second or third generations, they are still 'Puerto Ricans.' Fernando Ferrer, Ricky Martin, Mark Anthony, Jennifer López call themselves *boricuas* and Puerto Ricans, although they were born and raised in New York City, and their primary language is English. They have a tremendous pride in being Puerto Ricans. They feel totally Puerto Rican, exactly the same as those that were born and raised in Puerto Rico."

"That is an interesting argument that not all Puerto Ricans would agree with," he said.

I realized that it was time to finish the coffee break and get back to the office.

When I came back to the office, I had a message to call Professor Navarro from the University of Puerto Rico. She was organizing a conference in Puerto Rico on the topic of bilingual education and bilingualism, and she wanted me to give a presentation on the topic of *Puerto Rico: Two Languages for Everyone?* She mentioned that it could be presented in either language, Spanish or English since the audience was bilingual. I asked myself:

"In which language should I make this presentation-Spanish or English? What is it that my Puerto Rican colleague wants me to say at this upcoming conference? "Does Professor Navarro want me to talk about bilingualism and the role of English and Spanish in the Puerto Rican educational system or perhaps in New York? Does she want me to say that English is not for everyone in Puerto Rico? Does she want me to emphasize the need for Puerto Ricans to achieve, first, the mastery of their Spanish language? Does she want me to propose that English should be taught as a foreign language and not as a second language?"

Thinking about going to Puerto Rico energized me. I love my island: its mountains, waters, and people; a land tied to my childhood, my roots; my home that was with me through all my dreams, my successes, sad moments, and my many, many struggles. The breeze of the early mornings and early afternoons, the green countryside, the blue sky, the splendid moon and even the rainy cloudy days of Puerto Rico, all speak to my heart. I saw myself merging with my *compatriotas*, using the same strategies for daily survival in order to cope and psychologically confront the challenges of a weak economy, dependency on the United States, the 'made in China' materialism and the uncertain political climate and trajectory.

One month later, I went to Puerto Rico, to the UPR, where I delivered my lecture on *Puerto Rico: Two Languages for Everyone?* I said that there is a need to maintain and foster the growth of Spanish, the primary language of the island, and to promote the learning of English. Both languages play a unique and different role on the island. Puerto Ricans need to understand that students learn faster and better when the primary language is used as the medium of instruction. How many students learn English varies greatly, depending on many different factors. Some Puerto Ricans speak English well, others poorly or not at all. As a rule, those that have a high level of education or who live in the more sophisticated metropolitan areas of the island, where there is more contact with English speaking people, are more likely to be proficient in English than those in the more remote parts of the island or the poorer sections of the big cities. Bilingual individuals have the advantage of communicating with people from different cultures, having different perspectives on life, fostering an open mind, creating opportunities for a variety of jobs, and having the ability to read literature in the original text of either language. I also said that there was a need to provide students with better instructional conditions and more qualified teachers.

In general, the presentation was well accepted, although a small group of attendees stood up and told me to be careful about making general statements about bilingualism without understanding the political implications of proposing bilingualism for everyone in Puerto Rico. They said that bilingualism implies that Spanish and English play the same role in schooling and that cannot be- Spanish should be the only medium of instruction, and English should be taught as a foreign language. I thanked them for their thoughtful comments.

I returned to New York City and my job as a professor continued. There were good days, and there were challenging ones. Throughout the years, and especially in those years of turbulence and extreme challenges, I embarked on a search for healing practices. I explored yoga, Tai Chi, Reiki, meditation, and consultation of spiritual healers. These therapeutic practices and rituals are infused with African, Asian, and Christianity spirituality. For instance, spiritualist healers (espiritistas) use rosaries, light candles for and say prayers to saints, but they also recommend taking plant baths with white flowers and aromatic oils, and taking evil out by using *sahumerios* (putting myrrh and incense in a lighted charcoal). Usually the healer or *espiritista* provides services similar to that of psychotherapy. For example, they study problems and assign the cause to a spirit that emotionally afflicts an individual. The healer helps an individual get rid of the bad spirits and put her/him in contact with protective guiding spirits. The *espiritista* focuses mainly on personal problems (the husband that has another woman, the pregnant daughter, the lawsuit).

I visited Paula several times for a *consulta* (spiritual advice). Paula is a popular *espiritista* in el Barrio. When Paula, who was very convincing, talked about the afterworld power of saints and spirits in our lives, I wanted to believe that they could actually come to my rescue. I thought that I needed all the help that I could get from the divinities, the entities, or as Paula says, the "*seres*."

My *amiga* Fela introduced me to Paula, and since then, I always go to her. Paula is a good listener and a good motivator. At those moments when I feel down, I call her.

"*Dime, ¿qué está pasando?*" (Tell me what is happening?) she asks me.

"Paula, I need to see you," I say.

"*Mija, cuando tú quieras venir, yo estoy aquí.*" (Whenever you want to come, I am here.)

I make an appointment to see her as soon as I can get there, and when I arrive, she is waiting for me. Usually, she offers me coffee, which I always accept. We engage in a general conversation about the three children she adopted or about issues that are happening in her or my own family circle. Then, Paula tells me that I have two options: a *consulta*, or a card reading. Usually, I go for the card reading, and Paula, through the reading of the cards, helps me to express my feelings or frustrations, my struggles, or the identification of a problem that I am presently facing. Initially, I never tell Paula what the problem is that has taken me to her house. Through the conversation and the reading of a specific card, the problem comes out. She talks about the different dimensions of the problem and discusses ways of dealing with it. The *seres* (spiritual forces) guide Paula to help me with my problem. Usually, this is a one to two- hour conversation. She may give me a bath of white flowers to eliminate the negative forces, tell me to light a candle for "*Papa Bocó*" or "Saint Anthony," or she might take a red piece of cloth and pass it all over my body. When I leave Paula's house, I feel rejuvenated and *con ganas* to continue the daily struggles of my life. Before I leave, I put $21 on her dining table. Now, this is mental therapy!

Through yoga, meditation, and spiritual sessions I have found ways to cope and ultimately find pleasure and joy. The self- introspection and the reflection helped me to find peace in my soul. I began to do more things by myself, *sola*. I made mistakes, but I began to see mistakes as lessons. It was the process of knowing me. And for the first time, I saw that my failed marriage was a life lesson that I had to turn into a victory. Fortunately, I have tried to forget all these bad experiences, to eliminate the anger and resentment, and I have tried to look at the future with forgiveness and confidence. I remind myself that for many women, marriage does not work; they divorce, and they go on with their own lives. In fact, many divorced women use the separation experience to empower themselves and become stronger individuals.

I had the self-assurance and comfort that, in spite of all the struggles and sadness involved, there were positive outcomes. Today, I feel that I am a better human being than I was before. And I appreciate having these past experiences because they contributed to my self-assurance, my independence, and empowerment. When I am looking at the sunrise, I am relaxed, and I thank human kind and God for the beautiful setting. In other words, I am more appreciative of what is around me, of what I have, even if it is less than what I used to have. By closing and opening circles, I have been able to be ME, myself. I have the tranquility of a happy woman and I have learned to depend on myself. My friends tell me that they feel peaceful in my house, and that I transpire peace. And every time that I can, I recite this sentence: "I give thanks for what I have. I simply count the blessings from above."

I finished my three years of department chair, and then went back to being a professor. During those three years, I never stopped being coordinator of my program of Teaching English as a Second Language. I continued with my routine of teaching, service, and scholarly work. My students inspired me, and working with them, especially in the preparation of their doctoral dissertations was an incentive to keep abreast of what was happening in the field of education. I even taught in the summers, and after completing all the tasks required by my program, I usually went to Puerto Rico to re-energize. It was one of those mornings that I was walking through the beach of Isla Verde, that I received a phone call from the newly hired dean of the Graduate School of Education.

"*Doctora*, I need your help. I want you to accept my invitation to become Associate Dean for Academic Affairs."

"Why me?" I asked him.

He briefly explained that he had observed my working style and my ability to do things, (he was a member of the faculty for many years) and he needed someone to help him with the academic demands of the job. I accepted. I brought Lissette as my secretary in the Dean's Office.

I found that I was not really prepared for the demands of this administrative job. It was a never-ending job. There were many tasks attached to this job with no guidelines or information. Many of my colleagues never accepted me, although they were satisfied when tasks were accomplished. I found myself fighting battles alone. At meetings, I was constantly questioned about information or about my knowledge of certain procedures. The faculty would look me in the eyes with queries and their eyes remained *fijos* (direct) until they were given the requested information. At the beginning, I did everything to show them that I was knowledgeable and competent. But the preparation took many hours of my sleep. Many of my colleagues saw my office as the one responsible for solving all the problems of their programs and their students. With respect, I had to convey to my colleagues that the academic deanship was mainly to make the school academically efficient, but not necessarily to become a clerical problem solver. Lissette was also bombarded with trivial tasks that were not part of the dean's office.

One October, while I was in the office preparing for a week of meetings, document preparation, and local travel, I realized that there is nothing more beautiful in New York City than an afternoon at the end of October. The sky is the color of lavender; the leaves are multitude of yellows, oranges, and browns. I looked through the big window of my office, and I began to make plans to take some time off and meet with my *amigas*. This administrative job was a very demanding one, and I needed to reach outside the university for support.

Different from my early years, I always have a group of *amigas* surrounding me. My amigas are not only my friends, they have also become my sisters. They are a blessing of life, and keeping in touch with them is a wonderful medicine for loneliness and comfort. *Amigas* need each other to go out, to do things together, to share accomplishments and failures, and to remember special days in each other's lives. My *amigas* list is long: Aleyda, Ana, Aurea, Carmen, Chun, Evelyn, Elizabeth, Frances, Giselle, Griselle, Judy, Hilda, Luisa, María, Miriam, Nancy, Paquita, Paula, Oclides, Terry, Youn Soo; too many to list all of them.

When a woman has to walk the difficult and tumultuous valley of life, *amigas* are watching, and some of them may even be on the other side of the cliff waiting, hands always out- stretched as a sign of comfort, guidance, and help. *Amigas* drive in storms, on snowy or rainy days, during day or during night, if they feel that they are needed. *Amigas* back friends up when life produces deception, give advice on how to raise and educate children, provide beauty tips, give recommendations on professional issues, keep secrets, and help to get out of bad relationships. *Amigas* hear the *lamentos*/laments when a husband leaves, when a child gets sick, or when a parent dies. Time goes on, life goes on, distance becomes a barrier, children grow up and leave, love disappears, and hearts get broken, full-time work ends, parents die, colleagues forget other colleagues, men become indifferent; but *amigas* are always present. It does not matter the time and the distance between *amigas*, an *amiga* is never too far when she is needed.

Throughout the years, I have attended or organized social meetings with one, two, or three *amigas*. This social interaction has helped me to find a balance between being a professor and being a human being. My *amigas* and I have had the desire to share, to talk, and to listen. My *amigas* have different or similar opinions and feelings about varying topics and people, but what unites us is the desire to affirm our paths, and to support each other. A meeting with *amigas* is a lot of fun. It involves a lot of thinking aloud and reflecting about different topics. An *amiga* gathering is not for filling time caused by loneliness, because none of my *amigas* is "lonely," although many of them live alone. They see each other as a friend and as an adviser, because all of these women are strong individuals, and their histories and experiences are lively and interesting.

The therapy of meetings with my friends helped me during these months. One morning, I went to the dean and I informed him that I would be resigning as academic dean at the end of that academic year. He could not believe my words.

"Why?" he asked me again and again.

I explained that the stress of the job was making me very sick; I was anxious and my tinnitus was getting to intolerable levels. Reluctantly, he accepted my resignation. In April, to prevent rumors from among the faculty, I announced at a faculty meeting that for the reasons of illness, I was going to leave the deanship at the end of the year. Surprisingly, no one said a word.

At the end of July, the dean approved a one-semester sabbatical for me to recuperate. That semester the university president had invited the deans to send faculty recommendations for the appointment of distinguished professorships. The dean of the Graduate School of Education sent in my name.

Blending Teaching and Scholarship with Community Involvement

Xae Alicia Reyes

Xae Alicia Reyes is an associate Professor of Education and Puerto Rican and Latino Studies at the University of Connecticut. She has been described as a passionate community activist who blends teaching and scholarship with community involvement. She was born in Santurce, Puerto Rico and has baccalaureate and master's degrees from the University of Puerto Rico's Rio Piedras campus and a PhD from the University of Colorado at Boulder. She has taught at UPR- Rio Piedras and Cayey campuses, Syracuse University, Le Moyne College, the University of Colorado, and the Economics Institute in Colorado, Rhode Island College, and Brown University, and since 1999, at the University of Connecticut. Her passion for teaching has been a constant in her work. A recent note from a student read:

Dr. Reyes:

I have been wanting to write to you since Monday.

I went to my classes and met my professors. After having you as a professor, life is not the same. Needless to say…you are greatly missed.

I thought of Matt when he said he has never had a professor like you and just this whole week I have been thinking the same thing. (Female Student 2009)

Equity and social justice are mantras she lives and works by, so access to education is a core value which drives her teaching, scholarship and service. Her book *How the Language and Culture of Researchers affects their Choice of Subjects and Methods* (2005) is a collection of essays that questions the reliability of work that ignores the issue of transparency on the part of the researcher regarding their proximity to their subjects in a variety of contexts. This book reflects the questions and concerns Reyes has raised for much of her career when subjected to research and professional development activities where the researchers have no direct connections to their subjects and rely heavily on informants to obtain their data.

She has addressed teacher preparation concerns, media representations of Latinas and their impact on teaching and learning, and Latina experiences in higher education. Issues of language are reflected heavily in all of her work. In addition to teacher education, Reyes has taught Spanish, business and cross-cultural communication, qualitative research in multiethnic and multilingual settings and courses on Latinas in education. Her work has been published in the *Journal of Latinos and Education, Journal of Hispanic Higher Education, and the Latino Studies Journal.* In addition, she has contributed chapters to a number of books.

Often described as eclectic, Reyes is active in her church where she participates as a presenter on numerous topics related to spirituality and cultural diversity. She has been trained at the Mexican American Catholic Cultural Center in San Antonio. Since the year 2000, Reyes has also hosted a local Public Access show called Education Matters.

Reyes was recently awarded a Fulbright to visit Thailand as a Senior Specialist. There, she consulted on curriculum design with Burapha University International College's faculty, taught Social Communication, and assisted in the induction of a new faculty member through an apprenticeship model.

She is currently interim director of the Puerto Rican Latin American Cultural Center at the University of Connecticut.

Puertorra: ¿No Hablas Español?

Dices que eres muy puertorriqueña
de aquellos nacidos en la calle 112,
tus padres te dicen que sí eres boricua
que tu apellido es Rosado y Rodríguez
aunque no puedes pronunciar las erres.
Tu sangre mixta se calienta al oir la salsa
tu cuerpo lleva la cadencia latina
y sientes orgullo de tu herencia cruzada.
Te encanta el arroz con habichuelas rojas
comes la pana, el aguacate y los pasteles,
juegas dominó con la gente del barrio,
y sientes, sufres y lloras por tu gente
pero te preocupas porque no hablas español.

No te preocupes mi hermana boricua,
Tú, sólo tú debes definir tu identidad
nadie más puede o debe de juzgarte
ese es tu derecho único y legítimo,
de sentirte totalmente incluida y respetada
en la gran familia puertorra, la boricua.
Reclama tu poderosa identidad puertorriqueña,
no importa cuántas generaciones vengan
no importa tu acento, sino lo que Tú eres,
sino pronuncias la erre, sino hablas español
porque el ser puertorriqueña, amiga boricua,
va más allá de la barrera del idioma.

Chapter 11

THE INTERSECTION OF TWO CULTURES

At the end of the semester, I received the news that I had been appointed as the Aquaviva Distinguished Professor. As expected, my colleagues read the electronic and regular mail announcement made by the University President about my, and a few others' appointments of distinguished professors, and it was as if they never received the announcement. My colleagues saw me in the hall and in meetings, and never mentioned a thing. Only two colleagues out of forty-five congratulated me: Terry and Chun. On the day of the ceremony in which the President was going to present the distinguished professorship awards, few colleagues from my school came to the award ceremony; none of them sat near me, or even said "congratulations." Their behavior did not surprise me. Throughout my entire professorship journey I had to climb alone, working more than anyone else in the college and not taking any academic work or accomplishments for granted.

At the end of September, there was a ceremony where the President introduced the eight distinguished professors. A lunch followed the ceremony, and at both events, I sat with strangers because the few colleagues from the School of Education that came did not stay; they had to hurry to their small offices to accomplish very important tasks. One of those important tasks was to read their most recent e- mail. Later on, at the first school council meeting of the following semester, questions were raised concerning the criteria used by the president of the institution to determine appointments for distinguished professorships. My colleagues were so unsatisfied with the president's appointment that they even wrote to the Faculty Senate, questioning the criteria used for such appointments. The Faculty Senate, which is composed of representatives from all the university schools, also questioned the criteria used by the President in awarding the eight distinguished professorships. The Faculty Senate passed the following resolution:

> "An advisory committee appointed by the president of the Faculty Senate will receive nomination for internal or external candidates for Distinguished Professor. The Committee will review the nominations and solicit supporting materials from those nominees for Distinguished Professor it considers preeminent in their field, those with demonstrated exceptional achievement. After reviewing the complete nominations the committee will make recommendations to the President for the nominations of Distinguished Professors to the Trustees."

I believe that the President of the University was so frustrated with the noise made by the faculty that in subsequent years, there were no more distinguished professor appointments.

Several years passed since I received my distinguished professorship rank, and I was seriously thinking about retirement. I wanted to have the flexibility to do personal, recreational, and travel activities beyond the restricted university schedule. This thought led me to reflect on the two worlds that I have had and enjoyed: Puerto Rico and New York City. I have been at the intersection of two cultures, where the Caribbean meets the Atlantic Ocean; where the tropical weather is balanced with the cold days of the north. I identified my retirement date, and I searched for a home.

"Home" is a complicated issue for many Puerto Ricans in the United States. What does it mean to go "home" when the more recent home is part of the mainland United States and when there are also many heritage feelings about the island of Puerto Rico? I always said that I would retire to Puerto Rico. I continuously talked about the dream of being able to go and live permanently in *la isla del encanto* (the enchanted island). But when people become old and mature, they become more reflective and careful in making final decisions related to the place they retire. There are many other factors to consider: grandchildren, amigas' network, cultural activities, community attachments, and health facilities.

When I am in New York City, I miss Puerto Rico, and when I am in *la isla del encanto*, I miss the Big Apple. In Puerto Rico, I have sisters, nieces, and cousins, and in New York City, I have my sentimental partner, my son, two grandchildren, and most of my *amigas*. One thing that I know is that I would like to live near the beach and near the snow; in a tropical paradise and in a cold renaissance.

Today, although I live in the New York City area, I maintain close ties with the people of Puerto Rico, and especially with my close relatives. I try to visit the island three or four times a year. When I go, I share my time between the beach, the mountains, and the many beautiful areas of my island. I spend time in Puerto Rico, not as much as I want to, but enough to keep a sense of who I am.

I have been blessed with owning a small apartment in a condominium complex in Isla Verde, an area not too far from the airport. I love this place because its residents are mostly made up of retired Puerto Ricans, mainly from New York City and the island. There are also several Cuban professionals that fled Cuba during the Cuban revolution. The mixture of residents provides variances in the voices and stories circling in the building. This interaction with my island of Puerto Rico has always given me happiness and pleasure. I recall those days and imagine myself visiting my sister María, when she and I, would walk around her small piece of hillside land. María lives in a small house in a remote *barrio* of San Lorenzo, a small town in the northeast part of the island. When I visit her, I love to take the *toronjas*, the *panapén*, the *pana de pepita*, and the *naranjas* from the trees. The rising sun adds a crystal glow to my sister's smile as she takes an orange or a grapefruit from outside her house.

At one of those visits, while walking through María's land, I picked the best oranges, and I went with her to the kitchen to eat them. I peeled an orange while my sister prepared a meal for the family that had arrived. She began by frying *alcapurrias* (mashed green bananas with meat). Then, we opened a bottle of Lambrusco while Maria prepared *arroz con gandules* and boiled some pasteles that she had prepared the day before. While in the kitchen, I talked to her about some of our experiences growing up. She listened to me but kept busy with the cooking. Suddenly she said to me:

"Tú no sabes cocinar." (You do not know how to cook.)

Then, looking at the relatives that were sitting in the living room, next to the kitchen, María told the following story very loudly, so that everyone could hear.

"Let me tell you that, one day, Angela cooked a chicken soup that no one was able to eat. The soup had no taste."

My nieces, my sister Socorro, and my friend Aida smiled in an agreement.

"I suppose that is my reputation in the kitchen!" I responded.

While the food was cooking, María and I went around her garden. She showed me *yerba bruja*, the plant for ear pain; *yerba buena* and *ruda*, both plants good for stomach and ovary pain; *tártago* for good luck and to retire bad spirits; and *limoncillo*, a treatment for temporary colds. When we came back from exploring the herb garden, we sat at the table with a big plate; we ate *arroz con gandules* (yellow rice with peas) and *pasteles*. And, we had a second glass of Lambrusco. My sister continued describing the health benefits of her plants.

"You do not have to take any chemicals into your body," she said. "Plants are curative, if you know which ones to take."

"Well, sometimes you need to take those medicines prescribed by the doctors," I said.

"But very few of them. People take too many chemical medicines, and while they help you with one problem, they damage another part of your body. I say that people should try the herbal plants first, and if they do not cure them, then use the chemical ones," she replied.

After this exchange, she stood up and went into the living room corner to an old record player. She put on a long record with the songs of *Felipe Rodríguez, Chucho Avellanet, Ramito,* and *La Calandria*, all Puerto Rican singers from the 60s and 70s.

"Do you remember these songs?" she asked me.

"Of course," I replied.

In a way, I envy my sister because she has very little, however she is very happy with what she has and with herself. I have more than she has, and I am not always as happy as she is.

Two days later, I went to visit my other sister, Socorro, in Aguas Buenas, my hometown. Socorro lived in the same small house where I spent several of my teenage years. While visiting Socorro, I came back to my childhood years in this town of tall green mountains. Aguas Buenas exudes a sense of constancy of time, moving slowly, nestled in a mountain with the Cordillera Central, with idyllic temperature, and an image of changeleness. In this town, very few major events happen. Life is the same, day after day. With the exception of my sisters, today, no one knows me in this town.

I parked my rental car on one of the small streets, and I went to the plaza. The plaza was completely deserted due to TV, the location of *urbanizaciones*, or perhaps the tendency of people to go to the shopping malls, which are located in the outskirts of the big cities. These shopping malls displaced the role played by the central plaza in town, a feature of small town life, sadly lost in the urban sprawl of the capital city.

La Esquina Famosa, the town store where you could find every piece of clothing or home accessory, is still there. For a moment, I thought of going in and saying hello to Modesto, the owner. But I was afraid that he probably would not be there now. So many years had passed! I looked for the *Farmacia América*, an institution in Aguas Buenas, owned by the pharmacist's son who pursued a pharmacy degree and decided to marry and come back to the town to provide his services to the rich, as well as to the poor. I searched for the building, but instead, in the same place, I saw a video game store. The Catholic Church was still there, remodeled though. It is the same church where for two years, every morning; the nuns would take me and my classmates to mass before starting the school day. There were some new small shops in town, but almost everything else was the same. One quick inspection told me that Aguas Buenas was the same; however, *I was not the same*. I had changed. I am a Puerto Rican female professor who lives in New York City with a long list of memories and experiences.

Tears fell from my eyes, not out of sadness, but because the town that had shaped my personality and interests, and, in ways, was the root of so many of my life's struggles, had essentially remained unchanged. For one hour, I stayed immersed in my reflections. After that, I saw the bakery, I went inside and bought *pan de agua* (French bread) and several *mayorcas*, which are like big sweet doughnuts, and I headed to Socorro's house.

Her house is one block from the church and from the plaza. It is a small house surrounded by humble neighbors, and by stray cats and dogs that come every morning and every evening to be fed by my sister. She has taken on this mission so that these animals will not die of hunger. I sat in the small living room, sharing and tasting the *pan* and the *mayorcas* with Socorro's delicious coffee. And she told me the most recent news of the town.

"Marcelo and Petra died."

"William and Don Toño are very sick."

"The son of Genaro won the elections; Aguas Buenas is now part of the *Partido Popular*."

Visiting Puerto Rico and my family gave me the inspiration to continue to *face la lucha* (the struggles). My apartment on the island provides me with the comfort that although I reside in the mainland US, I have a piece of Puerto Rico in my hands.

One evening that week, I was sitting near the swimming pool of my apartment complex, and I heard a group of residents at "remembrance time" going back to the times when they were young and lived in places such as New York, Chicago, Boston, Philadelphia or in big houses in cities or towns of Puerto Rico.

"I was an engineer with a big house. My children are grown-ups and the three of them live in United States; one in Orlando, one in Maryland, and one in Dallas. I no longer need a big house. Also, I became afraid of muggings, so I decided to come here for more safety and security," I heard one of them saying.

I saw a second group under the palm trees that surround the complex building; they were sitting down in their beach chairs, having a beer or a glass of wine and talking about daily issues or news. This group was very careful about what they were saying, not to offend anyone in the group. Perhaps they represented different political, religious, and lifestyle voices. They did not talk about politics or religion but about the needs of the complex and the improvements it could use. They also expressed their unhappiness with the high incidence of domestic violence, drugs and car accidents on the island. I have noticed that during the weekdays, a group of men sit in the plastic chairs in the recreation room in front of the swimming pool, and play dominoes from early afternoon to early in the night.

The same day, a woman who was a resident, sat next to me in one of the pool seats, I said hello to her, and we engaged in a conversation. She mentioned to me that although she had lived on Tinton Street in the Bronx for 30 years, a "bad street" in the South Bronx, and there were days that she had no heat or hot water, she was still dreaming of those years that she spent on the mainland. She missed walking the streets, going to the Laundromat, preparing and selling pasteles around the neighborhood, and celebrating holidays such as Christmas and Thanksgiving with friends and relatives.

"I was never alone in New York," she said.

"But people say that New York is a very cold and unfriendly city," I said.

"Not for me. Even when I went to the bodega, I knew people who were shopping there, and we talked to each other. I also sat outside of the building, and I played dominoes with my friends."

"But you can do that here, too," I said.

"*Mija*, it is not the same. Here, people have social groups and you have to be careful of what you say because they can mention you and what you said," she said.

I looked to the farthest area of the complex and I saw another group. There were about eight ladies gathered together talking about the *acontecimientos del condominio* (events of the condominium).

"Do you know that the electric company shut off the electricity in apartment 404 because the people did not pay?"

"I was told that Emiliano is gay and that he brought his new boyfriend here."

With my eyes closed I heard all these comments from afar. I was not invited to join these private conversations or private activities. Two or three residents have asked me several times about my life and questioned me why I was not often seen in the building. I explained that I was residing in New York City. They looked at me and kept silent. I recognized that they have not accepted me as part of their inner circle of trusted residents. I understood them very well. I have no rush to be accepted by them, and I will probably never be a trusted neighbor. And I do not mind, as long as my neighbors allow me to sit there, near the palm trees where I can receive the *caricias del mar* (sea caresses).

I am always relaxed in Puerto Rico, especially in this enchanting apartment in Isla Verde. I call this place paradise, although it is a very humble apartment, and I would never change it for any other place in the world!

It was in one of my most recent visits to Puerto Rico that I attended a social gathering with a group of my amigas living in Puerto Rico. This get-together was at Luscinda's apartment in Torrimar, a condominium that overlooks the *Laguna del Condado* (Condado's lagoon). These are all professional women; some of them had lived in New York or New Jersey, and some of them had lived their entire lives on the island. They meet every month at a different house to see each other, to socialize, to eat and to drink together, but more importantly, to create a forum to express their experiences, readings, learning, and opinions about several topics, especially *"el Puerto Rico de hoy."* (the Puerto Rico of today). I am always invited, and if in Puerto Rico, I am always present at these gatherings. I learn so much from my *amigas* in Puerto Rico.

There were about 10-12 *amigas,* sitting in a semi circle, all of them with a glass of wine or beer. Although most of these women are bilingual, every time the group meets, Spanish is usually the language spoken. But when one monolingual English-speaking *amiga* joins the group, usually as a guest, English is used, although there are Spanish phrases and words that are preferred to be said in Spanish. The English speaking *amigas* are forced to learn to guess the meaning of these untranslated words or phrases.

"Bienvenidas! (Welcome!) There is so much information and news to share and talk about today. Anyone want to start?" Luscinda said at the gathering.

"Yes, I want to," Sonia began.

"Did you read in *El Nuevo Día* today about a group of Puerto Rican professionals that went to Washington to demand that Puerto Ricans have a voting voice in the US Congress? We have no vote and our voice is ignored. Puerto Rico is a conquered, occupied island, annexed to a homeland that demands acculturation to a dominant foreign nationality. This sense of belonging to someone else has reduced, to a certain degree, people's indigenous creativity and has inspired cultural resistance and syncretism," Sonia said.

"I agree with what you are saying," Maribel added, "and, I think that as Puerto Ricans, we need to continue to raise our voices here on the island and outside in Washington."

"Also, Puerto Ricans need to continue to identify themselves with the *jíbaro* traits of self-reliance, independence, love of the earth, and family connectedness," Sonia said.

" Aha," Rosalba said, "This sentiment of *puertorriqueñismo* needs to continuously be refreshed in the minds of those individuals who try to ignore it. "

"But uncertainty about the island's freedom or eventual merger with the United States constantly influences life, government, and politics in Puerto Rico," Sally added. "Puerto Ricans take politics extremely seriously; however, most of the time we do not address the real issues, especially those of our political destiny. "

"In Puerto Rico, everything is politics, especially the issue of status." I said. "Every Puerto Rican has an opinion, and this opinion identifies the island's political parties. People are passionate about deciding on the future of the island: they eat breakfast fighting or criticizing the opposing party, and when it is dinner or bed time, they are still commenting on the greatness of their party and the detriments of the opposing party. 'My party is better than yours,' and they go all the way, accepting as appropriate the behaviors of their own party, even if these behaviors are not acceptable ones."

"When the ex-governor of the island was accused of lying about providing information about past work experiences in order to get an increase in his retirement pension, a significant number of Puerto Ricans collected thousands of dollars so that he could return the money in question. Political ambivalence weakens a people's vitality- a price paid for their ethnicity's survival- a distinctive trait of residents in a colonized nation," Sonia replied.

"Let me give an example of that," Luscinda said. "Do you remember when in 1996, the United States Congress ended tax breaks for outside companies operating factories or managing money in Puerto Rico? The incentives for companies operating in Puerto Rico were phased out, bringing high unemployment and people's dependency on welfare services. And with the exception of the rich families that have investments in food processing and real estate, local controlled business is mostly limited to professional and personal services."

"But not everyone in Puerto Rico shares the money equally," Ruth mentioned. "I read that the top 10 percent of Puerto Ricans receives about 35% of Puerto Rico's income, 50% of the population on the island is middle class, which is made up of people with a steady full-time job. The additional 15% of Puerto Rico's income is shared by almost 40% of the Puerto Rican population, many of whom receive public assistance for survival."

At this time, Luscinda stopped the conversation and asked everyone to go to the buffet table and enjoy *paella* with *tostones* and salad.

Once the food disappeared and the *amigas* were eating the delicious *flan*, the conversation opened again.

"I want to go back to the conversation we were having," Maribel said. "Due to this Puerto Rican political and economic ambivalence, Puerto Rico is always in a state of survival. For this reason, there are movements or actions to be taken when other nations or individual groups try to take ownership of our land. For example, Puerto Ricans' involvement stopped a huge mining project that would have removed minerals from the island. Another group's movement persuaded the United States to withdraw its Navy from Culebra and Vieques, two islands belonging to Puerto Rico that were used as US military bombing site. The people's demonstrations made the government aware of the serious environmental damage, health risks, and poison emissions into the island's air."

"But I have to add something else," I said. "In spite of all the calamities and abuses mentioned by some of you before, in Puerto Rico, there is a tremendous desire for individual success and achievement. Many Puerto Ricans tend to be the best in their fields, and in their jobs. This is reflected in the way they dress, their hair treatments, customized cars, and decorated homes. When I visit these Puerto Rican middle class households, I am amazed at how much these individuals do with a very low salary. Their houses have the latest furniture and electronic equipment, and are generally technologically advanced. In addition, these families travel frequently, eat out, and go to expensive entertainment functions. As Puerto Ricans, we need to feel proud of our individual accomplishments."

"I do not totally agree with you," Carmen said. "Puerto Ricans may have accomplished many things, but we could do more and better. We need to work harder. Also, there are too many *noveleros* (curious people) in Puerto Rico. If the tall boats arrive in the port, all *noveleros* come to see these boats *para que no le cuenten* (so that no one has to tell them), even if getting there costs them time and money. If a Puerto Rican becomes a sport champion or a *Miss Universo*, all Puerto Ricans go to the airport to welcome and congratulate him or her. If the urban train is inaugurated and offers free trips, all Puerto Ricans come and try the ride, although you will never see them ride the train again. If Martin Luther King Day is celebrated on a Tuesday, Puerto Ricans take the previous Monday off, and they fill the beaches and the recreational areas. If their favorite political party has a demonstration, Puerto Ricans spend one tank of gas in order to join the *caravana* and the *mitin* (caravan or meeting)."

"But that is a natural behavior of many societies," I said. "Despite many signs of Americanization, public use of Spanish has improved and become the norm for communication. Moving toward a defense of the Puerto Rican ethnicity, creative literature written in Spanish has vastly expanded to portray human behavior, including new lifestyles in family and interpersonal relations. Novels, poetry, drama, art, and film have followed Latin American trends. English is seen merely as a resource for dealing with monolingual English speakers, especially in the trading and commercial areas."

At this point, exhausted by the many topics discussed, the many different points of view and the lateness of the night, the group decided to break up. I went back to my apartment, and began to put my belongings in my small suitcase because the next day, I was returning to New York City, and I was leaving the sun, the sea, and the sand.

A comment that I often heard from individuals who have visited Puerto Rico is:

"I will always remember two main aspects of your land: the weather and the people."

These are also the two elements most missed by Puerto Ricans who leave the island. I agree that the political, social, and economic pressures and challenges of the island have not changed the idiosyncrasies of Puerto Ricans. Puerto Ricans believe in themselves, and they are in a constant struggle to maintain their roots and heritage. At the same time, they are not very much interested in saving or working toward the future. They enjoy today, and think that *mañana* is "another day." Their hospitality to foreigners is unique; they share what they have without asking for anything in return. In addition, they know how to use their imagination, although they are timid in expressing themselves. On the other hand, they are extremely *vanidosos* (foppish) and proud of their land and their heritage.

Puerto Ricans are continuously and constantly struggling for their autonomy and self-sufficiency, and at the same time, they show an extraordinary desire to continue with American consumerism. I can see that Puerto Ricans are in the middle of a big dilemma: they want to keep their heritage and their language, but on the other hand, they are always imitating the daily life of the United States. Paradoxically, Puerto Ricans have denied giving up their Spanish ancestry, but have agreed to follow a series of American economic practices. That is why Puerto Rico is an island of many reforms, many forums, many voices, and many unaccomplished projects. The McDonalds, Burger Kings, Macys, JC Penneys, Home Depots, Wal-Marts, and Costcos are always crowded, and people and the government live in constant debt to pay for all this continuous American consumerism.

The renowned writer and educator, Antonio Pedreira, recognized all these behaviors and attitudes as negative ones. On the contrary, I see them as survival strategies that allow Puerto Ricans to endure in a society of doubt and uncertainty.

If I could, I would change certain things about Puerto Rico: Oh yes! I would make the island 15 degrees cooler, I would eliminate the direction of the winds-more toward the northeast (to change the route of the hurricanes), and I would make the island greener than it is today. I would stop the factories of cement and the building of *urbanizaciones*. I would make people less politically polarized, especially after the elections. And of course, I would stop those constant political demonstrations that make people too emotional to discern between "*mi ídolos*" (*my* heroes) of my political party, and the real issues concerning the well-being of the entire population. I would have people celebrate Puerto Rican holidays only, providing more working days for the benefit of the entire Puerto Rican society. But even if I cannot change these things, I will still love Puerto Rico as it is, and adore my Puerto Rican roots and heritage.

On one of those back and forth trips between Puerto Rico and the Big Apple, I sat on the plane next to a Puerto Rican lawyer, Licenciado Eliezer Navarro, who was going to New York City to meet a client. While the flight attendants were preparing the plane for take off, Licenciado Navarro and I engaged in a conversation where I mentioned that I had spent one month in Puerto Rico, and that I was glad to be headed back to New York City.

"Are you sure that you are happy to go back?" he asked me.

"Yes, I am," I said. "It has been characterized as an unfriendly and cold city; however, once you live there, there is a magical attraction. Yes, Manhattan is mainly tall buildings, assembled in a diversity of shapes and forms. Although, the other boroughs- the Bronx, Queens, Brooklyn, and Staten Island have some tall buildings, the majority of their construction is made up of small buildings and one or two-family houses "

"What can you say about the people that live there?" Licenciado Navarro asked me.

And I said:

"The population of New York City is diverse in ethnicity, age, language, and class. No one looks the same: the city is home to large groups of Chinese, Koreans, African Americans, Arabs, Jews, Latinos, Indians, and many Europeans. As you know, there are many Puerto Ricans living in all of the five boroughs. New York City is a cultural mosaic, a multiethnic city: Chinatown, Little Italy, the mosques, the Indian temples, Washington Heights, and el Barrio. These cultural networks serve to bring stability, security, and friendship that contrast the indifference of many other residents of the city. And this cultural and linguistic diversity provides a sense of belonging to all who live there."

"I heard that el Barrio is not Puerto Rican anymore," he said.

"That is true; gentrification is bringing many other groups to el Barrio. There are many Dominicans and Mexicans, but also White folks. Puerto Ricans are widely scattered throughout New York City, despite a noticeable concentration in certain areas such as el Barrio and the South Bronx. Early Puerto Rican arrivals chose El Barrio as their place of residence, choosing to live in the midst of their own people. Later on, they spread out to other areas."

"Why do you like this unfriendly city?" he asked.

"Personally, I like the informality of a big city as well as the diversity of cultures and the interaction of all these groups. It is amazing that the differences of these cultures, not their similarities, are what get people together. You learn to respect, appreciate, and value this diversity. When in New York, I am always trying to discover something new from this cultural and linguistic mosaic."

"But I have read that when an individual arrives for the first time, and has no friends or relatives in the city, that the city looks grayish and cold," Licenciado Navarro said.

"Yes, this is the first impression that I had of the city when I first came. I felt lonely and lost, and I was not able to make immediate social encounters with the people around me. With the years, through my jobs, both in public schools and at the university, through memberships in professional organizations and with my students, I was able to develop an extensive network. New York City became the place for meeting people, for social gatherings, for work, as well as for social enjoyment. I have met wonderful human beings who later on became part of my inner circle," I continued:

"In this city, one can have very stressful encounters and experiences. This has been a city of waves upon waves, of new immigrants, driving the city onward. Struggle and change have the city on its toes. The city is great because destiny never allowed it to take a rest. Effort and energy, challenge and striving has drawn from the city's mind and soul a constant burst of creativity, imagination, and drive that has made it what it is."

"Due to the competitive economy, everyone appears to be in a 'conquer mode and mood,' fighting to meet their own personal needs. Going to work is a sense of accomplishment. I admire working people who during those stormy and cold days, go out early in the morning to go to work. In addition, the continuous change in weather provides a sense of hope and *mañana*, something that Puerto Ricans rarely find on the island. Looking at New Yorkers, I see contented faces accepting the reality and struggles of daily life in the City. Taking the crowded subway and touching the bodies of unfriendly riders, has made me stronger than I was before. I have to hustle, and push in order to get inside the train, to then usually spend 45 minutes standing and sharing a suspended bar with several strangers. But after walking up the stairs and rushing into the crowded streets of Manhattan, I know I will finally arrive to the place of destination. If that place is the New York State Education Department at 32nd street, I welcome the building. Once I am inside, I look for the room and there, I find a seat, and I see people that I know and who I can talk to."

"I do not expect anything from anyone, and I am always in a survival mode. Going to public government offices is sometimes traumatic, but exciting at the same time. The staff may be indifferent to my problem, but I prepare myself in advanced. I have all and more of the necessary documentation and I expect the attendant to be unfriendly or indifferent. However, I do not accept 'no' for an answer, and I keep insisting until I get what I went there to get."

"Do you feel safe in New York City?" Licenciado Navarro asked.

"New York City is known as a crowded city- too many people walking its streets. In spite of the crowds, I always feel safe in New York City. I have never been mugged. However, I always look around as I walk, with my bag very secure in case someone follows me and wants to take something away from me. It is not out of fear, but the accumulation of survival skills that I was able to master living in this city."

"But the city has not been good for Puerto Ricans; *No les ha ido muy bien*," Licenciado Navarro said.

"There is a diversity of Puerto Ricans in New York City. There are the poor, the professional, the businessmen and women, as well as those that have mixed with other ethnic groups. Father Joseph Fitzpatrick, a well-know Jesuit sociologist, who always defended Puerto Ricans, mentioned that New York City is 'the largest Puerto Rican city.' The problem has been that Puerto Ricans uprooted themselves from a life they once took for granted, then found themselves as strangers in a life they do not understand. The values are different, the norms are no longer consistent, and life becomes confused. This confusion shakes the framework on which Puerto Ricans' lives were built.

"I read that many Puerto Ricans need to fight to maintain their identity against the disappearance of bilingual education and Spanish, and the push for students to learn English as soon as possible," Licenciado Navarro said.

"Yes, it is true to some extent. In New York City, the Spanish language is a symbol that distinctly identifies the Puerto Rican community. And they try to maintain the Spanish language, and many want schools to help their children to preserve this language. For these Puerto Ricans, the Spanish language is a symbol of identity, along with its social and cultural functions. The Spanish language is the symbol of that network of interaction, which is the basis for identity security. The use of Spanish opens the community to them, and immediately identifies them as 'one of our own.' But keep in mind that there is another group of Puerto Ricans that were born and raised in New York City and who do not speak Spanish; and they feel that they are as Puerto Rican as you and I."

"Why do Puerto Ricans not learn English?" Licenciado Navarro asked.

"Your assumption is not quite accurate. Puerto Ricans in New York City, for the most part, are proficient in English; in fact, most of them are bilingual. While they are proficient in both languages, they have a preference for speaking Spanish among themselves as a manifestation of the strength of the Puerto Rican community, as a sense of a clear identity."

"Some say that the Puerto Ricans of New York City, the *Newyoricans,* are different from the Puerto Ricans of Puerto Rico," Licenciado Navarro stated.

"To some extent I agree with that statement, although it is not entirely true. Puerto Ricans who moved to New York City to a new culture and language, eventually passed through a process of cultural assimilation. For example, they learned the English language, adopted the essential values of the larger society, and followed normal behavior patterns. At the same time, they retained an identity of their own as a community, preserving those particular values which distinguish them and which they cherish. These Puerto Ricans are closely tied with the strengths of their community, constantly asking themselves, 'who am I? To whom do I really belong?'

"After living in New York City for several years, Puerto Ricans begin to feel comfortable in this complex city, in spite of the many inconveniences, prejudices, and lack of opportunities for unskilled individuals. In New York City, you are just a Puerto Rican, and not necessarily identified with a political party. And, although you may identify yourself as a Democrat or a Republican, in the long run, you are still a Puerto Rican."

After these three hours of constant dialogue and expression, the pilot announced that the plane was landing at John F. Kennedy airport in New York City. I was coming home. While the plane landed I thought:

"It is important that Puerto Ricans, whether in Puerto Rico or in the United States mainland continue to have a strong sense of identity and belonging. Puerto Ricans belong to a community that is strong, self-respected, and self-assured. Language, social group, and organization of social and political life make up the institutional framework that gives identity and strength to this community."

A Leading Educator and Advocate

Nilda Soto Ruiz

Professor Nilda Soto Ruiz has dedicated her professional career to providing quality educational programs in both public and private educational settings, with more than 30 years experience as a teacher and high ranking administrator in the New York City Public School System. Dr. Soto Ruiz's accomplishments have distinguished her as a leading practitioner and advocate in the field of education. Her research interests include the teaching of English Language Learners and students with special needs.

Professor Soto Ruiz, who was born in New York City and is of Puerto Rican ancestry, is a product of New York City Public Schools. She earned a baccalaureate degree from the City College of New York. She received her master's and doctoral degrees from New York University.

Professor Soto Ruiz has serviced students in New York City at all grade levels. She has also assumed administrative positions at the district level in the Bronx and at the Central level. Among the numerous positions she has held are: Director of Bilingual Education, Chief Executive for Instruction, and Superintendent for the Office of Monitoring and School Improvement. She has shared her expertise by educating future teachers and administrators at Hunter College, the College of New Rochelle, and New York University. She was appointed by Governor Pataki to serve as a member of the Board of Trustees of the City University of New York, where she served for ten years. She was chair of the board's Committee on Academic Policy, Program, and Research and vice chair of the Committee on Fiscal Affairs. She also worked on public school and university collaborative programs during her tenure as trustee.

In 2002, Professor Soto Ruiz joined the faculty of Touro College as program chair for the programs in school administration, and she restructured the program which prepares administrators to work in public and private school systems. She retains a strong commitment to sharing her expertise to prepare students of diverse backgrounds to excel academically, and become leaders in education.

Praise the Day that Carries You Over

Clement G. London

It is not for us to say
What is the day today!
For it really matters not
How important it is or what
Name is assigned the day;
We should welcome today
Come what may!

Shouldn't we be grateful
For the chance to see today?
Yes, and to know how kind
A day has been or can be,
For the thought of being here
To see it against the alternative to
Sharing another world elsewhere?

Perhaps it is more important
To care instead how we fare,
In interacting with fellow humanity
Struggling against much difficulty
As we trudge through our life space
On the journey of human destiny.

So what matters it anyway, if
We know what day is today?
It still remains the tomorrow
That we worried about yesterday!
Then, *shun* the arrogance that may say
"Please go ahead and make my day!" Instead,

Be as grateful and mindful as ever
To praise the day that carries you over!

Chapter 12

TODAY IS A SPECIAL DAY

After 33 years as a New York City college professor, I finally made arrangements to retire. A retirement dinner was organized by Terry, a colleague and friend, and by Lissette, my loyal former secretary. Two weeks before the retirement dinner, Lissette called me up.

"*Doctora*, I am putting together the program for your retirement dinner, and I want to know how many minutes you need for your speech."

I sat down at the computer and drafted several pages of unrelated topics and thoughts. I wrote about this *jibarita*, who was born in the mountains of Aguas Buenas, who was a rural teacher in one of the most remote schools in Puerto Rico, and who traveled the long journey up to a distinguished professorship in New York City. Although I survived financial hardships, as well as professional and health challenges, I was satisfied with myself and with my journey. I had been completely devoted to my profession as a college professor. On many occasions, because I tried to be Mother Theresa, trying to solve all the issues and problems of my profession, I stayed late on the job, thinking that by doing the work that night, it would be better and easier for all the other individuals involved. I kept going, moving, traveling, making it to every possible meeting, and accepting jobs that no one else wanted because I felt a sense of responsibility and commitment to my profession. I thought that it was my responsibility to take on all these tasks. I never questioned my role in the undertaking of presentations, publications, meetings, clerical tasks, or being a professional source of information. I never questioned whether I was happy or unhappy with myself, because I saw these tasks as a job to be done. I was always satisfied to attempt and complete the many professorial and academic tasks that I had in front of me.

I was also committed to my family. When my three children were growing up, I spent time with them, choosing and monitoring their schools, supervising homework, evaluating their academic growth, buying and washing their clothing, providing them with religious beliefs, piano lessons, sports, and leisure trips. After working the whole day, I came home, and I made sure that my children were fed and cleaned, and that homework was completed and that they had sufficient sleep and rest to confront the next day of school. Once I made sure that they were in bed, I sat at my desk or computer, and then, I engaged myself in academic work for the university, for professional organizations, or for consultation jobs. I worked very hard. Everything called for effort, hard work, dedication, and faith in myself. And I did it with enthusiasm.

"No, these were not the appropriate reflections to say at a retirement dinner," I said to myself. "My friends, my students, my colleagues, and the administrators attending the event want to hear a more philosophical and less personal speech." And I started to draft it.

The day of the dinner, after all the congratulations and thanks I received from colleagues, friends, family members and former and active students, I spoke to the audience:

"I thank the administration of this university, for providing me the opportunity to teach and be able to prepare teachers, who will then teach children and youth. I am so proud of having the opportunity to prepare bilingual teachers, as well as English as a Second Language teachers. Bilingual teachers promote the development of their students to the extent of each child's potential, using first, the language students know best, and creating an atmosphere in which children or adolescents feel confident in themselves and in their ethnic and linguistic background. ESL teachers use a unique method to teach English, integrating language and content. These two disciplines compliment each other, and have become the fastest and best ways to educate culturally and linguistically diverse students in the United States. These disciplines prepare teachers to instill in their students a pride in their own language and culture, and an understanding and respect for other cultures and languages, especially the English language."

"I am also glad that I was able to have the opportunity to work with doctoral students in guiding them through the difficult process of completing a doctoral dissertation."

"I also thank my colleagues for joining me in some of my scholarly projects and for supporting me on those that I did alone."

I finished my speech saying that if given the opportunity today of restarting my professorship journey, "I would do it exactly the same way."

A year passed since I formally retired, and I found myself spending more time *sola* (alone), by myself, especially while writing these memoirs and working on small educational projects. In the midst of this work, I suddenly had the need to socialize with my New York City *amigas*. I looked at the calendar; then I called them up for a social gathering in my house in the Bronx. Fortunately, most of my amigas were in the city, and they accepted my invitation.

In preparation for my *amigas'* visit, I prepared two appetizers: shrimp in sauce and guacamole with chips. For dinner, I cooked *arroz con gandules, pernil*, baked chicken, and *tostones* with garlic sauce. I prepared my own *sangría* and I had beer and several bottles of wine. My *amigas* brought different types of desserts.

We sat down, and listening to Latin jazz and salsa, we began brainstorming some of the issues that preoccupied us as Latinas, and as professional women.

"I am glad that you invited us. It is wonderful to see friends that I haven't seen for a long time," Mary said.

"Thanks, I'm glad you came," I said. "We are not young anymore, and many of us are afflicted by illness, spending a lot of time at the doctor's office. I suddenly had the desire to see all of you, so I thought of planning this get-together. Life is short, and we have to take advantage of today and of our friendship."

"You are right about that," Carmen said. "For this reason, I try to take one day at a time, as if today is the last day of my existence. At this age, life has told me to be cautious and thankful of what I have and of what I accomplished. Preoccupations and worries aside, life is short and we do not know what will happen tomorrow. This is a new philosophy for me, a new way of looking at life. "

"I have the same philosophy," Rita mentioned. "Throughout the years, women are taught to be attached to something or to someone. First the parents, then the husband, the children, or a relative such as an aunt or a grandparent. Attachment can also be with a house, a job, the church, a hobby, or a sport. However, like Carmen, I realized that in doing all these things, I abandoned myself; I did not take care of 'me'- the most important individual in my whole circle. I was not making a balance between work, family, the social commitments, and my internal me."

"There is a magic word: *balance*," I said.

"I came to the conclusion that every human being needs to make a balance in life so that the mind is clear, powerful, and able to process thinking and implement actions so *that* we are empowered to be happy," Aida said. "I realized that I am the only one who can take the necessary steps in order to have physical and mental health, and overall life enjoyment."

"Well," I said, "today could be my last day on this beautiful land, and I have to take advantage of it. I realize that every individual has to look for ways to reach happiness and peace. As a Puerto Rican, as a woman, and as a college professor, I have strived for these. I make every possible effort to be happy. This reunion is one of these efforts."

"But what is happiness? How do you define this word?" Lissette asked.

"Happiness is being content and satisfied with yourself and with your surroundings, having the desire to live, and gaining satisfaction from daily life encounters," Lucy said. "It is getting up every day and saying: 'Life is wonderful!' In other words, happiness is the balance of body and mind, which brings mental peace and satisfaction to daily living and life."

"An important component of a woman's journey is her emotional well-being," Sally said. "The mind plays an important role in the happiness of an individual. It is well documented that women show a higher level of emotional afflictions than men: anxiety, panic, phobias, changes of mood, and depression. Sometimes these emotional problems are part of hormonal changes, and other times are caused by social and emotional factors that provoke stress, anxiety, and physiological changes such as high blood pressure and heart problems."

"I have had a very sensitive mind: *todo me preocupa* (everything worries me)," I said. "For example, several years ago, I had a meeting with the new division chair at my university with the purpose of providing recommendations for a new and better structure for the division. The night after the meeting, I went to bed, and I could not relax enough to be able to sleep. I spent all night developing several plans to come up with a solution to the issues we had discussed at the meeting. As you can see, I carry others' problems on my shoulders, and most of the time, these problems go into my lower back and manifest into my tinnitus."

"Same here. My mind is always *cargada*, full of preoccupations," Veronica said. "In addition, I take my responsibilities very seriously. I tend to do everything today, and not leave anything for tomorrow. For this reason, I feel a constant pressure of every day struggles, preoccupations, and challenges. Does this sound familiar? I am not surprised. Why do women have to be like this? I think it must be part of womanhood."

"I remember at one time that I was feeling down for no apparent reason. You may say that I was depressed," Miriam mentioned. "And I kept asking myself: 'Why am I feeling this way? I do not have any financial, family, or emotional problems.' But that general unhappiness with life kept coming back again and again."

"When that happens to me, I turn to one or two of my survival strategies," I said. "I become the cause of my own happiness. One of the first strategies that I used years ago was to write a list of those things that bring me happiness or satisfaction in life. I asked myself: What are the things that bring enjoyment to my life? I then wrote the answers that came to my mind. At that time, the list had items such as: being with my family, spending time with my friends, exercising three times a week, traveling with my partner, teaching at the university, traveling with my children, writing articles on topics of interest to me, being with my partner, writing poetry, having pieces of Three Kings art, listening to music, attending theater shows, collecting miniatures of cats, working in my garden, collecting porcelain dolls, spending a day with my grandchildren, and being with my sons and daughter. I typed the list and made several copies, and I put it in several places at home and at the office where I could see it. Looking at the things that make me happy, I tried to do or practice them."

" I still constantly use this strategy. The list changes or modifies according to the circumstances. In those moments of anxiety, frustration or lack of sleep, I read it and say: "If it is none of the above, it should not be important. I need to do something about how I am feeling."

"I always use this list, and go back to it to see what is missing in my life. And, if what is missing is not having my grandchildren near me, I pick up the phone, and I call one of my children and I set a time to see him or her. If I find that my children are too far from me, I make arrangements to have a social gathering with them in my house. If what I feel is some sense of distance from my partner, I call him up and I invite him to do something with me. After I engage in one of these activities, I feel much better. I do not expect someone to do something for me, but I try to do something enjoyable for myself, and when it is not there, I find a way to make it accessible to me."

"I use another strategy," Carmen Gloria said. "If I have a problem, or if I have a difficult situation in front of me, I look at the negative aspects of the situation and I try to change them to positive ones. For example, rather than saying 'I have to go to a meeting where I do not know anyone, therefore the meeting will be a disaster for me," I say: 'this is a good opportunity to meet new professionals who may bring me an additional professional perspective.' If I have a medical appointment I say: 'Everything is going to be fine.' And most of the time, it comes out that way."

"Yes, that is positive thinking," Lucy said. "Let me share a strategy that I use. Lately, I do not remember all of my dreams; there are those that make an impression on me. If I have one of these dreams, first thing in the morning, while I am still drinking my first cup of coffee, I begin to write down the dream and I usually finish with a personal reflection as to why I had the dream and what it really means to me. Rather than seeing dreams as negative, I see them as positive mental messages. And my reflections are usually positive reflections such as; 'the dream is telling me to check the tires and brakes of the car before driving it,' or 'there are people up there in heaven that are trying to send me a message about taking care of a family member that is in need of help.'"

"Are you hungry?" I asked.

Everyone applauded. We stopped our reflections to walk around the house, to go to the bathroom and to eat. However, while eating, the conversation did not stop. Amigas kept mentioning strategies for better living and for coping with daily struggles.

Retirement brings choices of what to do and when to do it. Retirement gave me the opportunity to expand my world; to research topics not related to education, to travel without having to attend a conference or to present an academic paper. The following experience is one of those 'extra professorial ones.' Through Satsavia, a spiritual therapist, I met an extraordinary healer, Joao Teixeira de Faria, better known as John of God. He is a Brazilian healer who works with different spiritual entities to help to alleviate human beings' physical and mental illnesses. My first experience with John of God was in Rhinebeck, New York, a place that he has visited several times. After seeing him, I became interested in visiting his town of Abadiania, the village that hosts his sanctuary's healing center. So, I went to Abadiania, which is located in central Brazil, one and a half hours from Brasilia. John of God's sanctuary is named *Casa De Dom* Inacio, in honor of Saint Ignacio de Loyola, the founder of the Jesuit Catholic order. Abadiania sits 1,000 meters above sea level on one of the largest crystal plateau in the world. John of God was guided to build his healing sanctuary here by the spirits that work through him, perhaps for the added power of earth's natural resources that may serve as power points to intensify healing energies.

During the two weeks that I was in Abadiania, I witnessed John of God seeing several hundreds of people three times a week at the Casa De Dom Inacio. He had sessions in the morning and in the afternoon, and did not charge a fee. I saw buses from all over Brazil filled with people seeking healing or wishing to pray or meditate on the crystal plateau. Others came to express gratitude for having already been healed, to cleanse and recharge and give themselves as mediums to support John of God's work. John of God welcomes people from all over the world, from all areas of life and beliefs, with many different types of diseases, or simply with a thirst for spiritual connection and transformation. I met some doctors, professionals, and healers in pursuit of healing or conducting research on John's work in Abadiania. It was truly a joy and a wonderful opportunity to visit John of God in this special place, and to feel the benevolent forces of love and faith rippling through the area. I experienced shifts in consciousness and a reconnection to a deep profound opening of the heart.

After returning from Brazil I had the desire to engage in activities for relaxation. One of those activities is to listen to Latino music. Many women use music to '*levantarse el ánimo*,' (get their spirits up), to receive a sense of happiness and hope, and to conquer loneliness and fear. Music has therapeutic results and can be an antidote against stress. It helps individuals to concentrate on rhythm and words; through this process the mind is engaged and the stress level is reduced. Women that suffer from an illness tend to forget that they are sick when in the presence of music. It has been found that music provokes physical changes in human bodies, altering body temperature, patterns of cerebral sound, and stress hormones in the blood. It also modifies heart rates and blood pressure.

I always kept a small radio in my office, and even when I was reading e-mails or correcting student papers, I had music on the background. This was usually instrumental music, especially Latin jazz, *boleros*, and salsa. In my home, I play my CDs all the time, a combination of Latino and American music.

I also practice meditation which provides me with comfort, peace, and hope.

It has been said that those who meditate daily have fewer propensities for getting sick, and they also recuperate quickly from sickness and surgery. I have also found that human beings become happier when they start to forgive each other. It is called 'the ability to close doors.' The closing of doors was popularized by La Lupe, the famous Cuban salsa singer, who sang a beautiful song that goes: "*Lo que pasó, pasó, y ya*" (what happened happened, and that's it). I think that no one and nothing is indispensable- not a person, not a place, not a job. Nothing is so important to continue spending life suffering because it was lost it, or because we never accomplished or acquired it. Closing doors means to move on to another page, to another circle.

I do not consider myself a religious individual, although I see myself as a 'spiritual being.' And within that spiritual context, I welcome several religious forces. At times, I attend Catholic mass, but if a friend invites me to an evangelical service, I happily go. If my Jewish friend asks me to attend the synagogue for a special service, I go, and I feel comfortable participating in the service. Occasionally, I attend an *espiritista* session and go for card readings. All of these activities give me peace and confidence.

I like to think that today is a special day. Today, I am happy with the way that I am. One day, an amiga sent me the following anecdote:

A friend of mine opened his wife's underwear drawer and picked up a silk paper wrapped package. "This," he said, "isn't an ordinary package." He un-wrapped the box and stared at both the silk paper and the box. "She got this the first time we went to New York, 8 or 9 years ago. She never put it on. She was saving it for a special occasion. Well, I guess this is it."

He got near the bed and placed the gift box next to the other clothing he was taking to the funeral home. His wife had just died. He said to me: "Never save something for a special occasion. Every day in your life is special."

People, including me, spend too much time thinking and feeling unhappy about the way that they look, aging, the food they eat, and the way they spend their time. But I remind myself that I have to live today as happily as I can. One way I do this is by saying *'today is a special day.'* And, not keep anything from bringing laughter and joy to my life. Today, I try to enjoy every day more than the day before, and be less involved with the responsibilities of the profession, the chores of the house, and other personal responsibilities. I no longer save anything new. I use crystal glasses every day. I wear all my clothes- the new ones and the fancy ones. I do not wait for someone to bring me flowers; I buy flowers for myself whenever I want them. I do not save my more valuables perfume or my jewelry for special occasions; I use it whenever I want to.

Happiness comes from within, not from hoping, but from being, recognizing the positivity around me. When it was discovered that I have tinnitus, I thought that it was the end of the world. I even stopped seeing my doctor because he played down the seriousness of the illness. After leaving his office with this ringing in the ear, he never called me up to see how I was coping. However, after several years with this condition, I have found ways to deal with it. For example, if I am involved in mental activities such as reading, writing, talking, or listening to music, I momentarily forget or feel that I have this illness. I do not remember that I have tinnitus, and the ringing in my ears temporarily disappears. I keep thinking that I cannot lose the happiness that I have sought so arduously.

I often think about the group of Latina professors out there that are trying to be successful and happy. How do these women support each other in contributing to their self-being, development, and happiness? As Latina professors, we have a sense of urgency to support other women, especially our own. We need to continue the struggle to succeed, to survive, and excel in academic communities.

We need to work hard to be, not only one of the best, but the best. I want to see many more Latina distinguished professors. I also want to see more Latinas show the kinship of their hearts and look positively at the world. With kinship, love, and faith, we empower ourselves, so that collectively, Latinas cannot be denied happiness and success, in spite of living and working within communities of resistance.

A Visionary Profesor

Milagros Marrero Díaz

Milagros Marrero Díaz has been a professor in the Occupational Therapy (OT) Department of the University of Puerto Rico at Humacao since 2003. Professor Marrero Díaz earned a Master's degree in Public Health and two professional certifications in Early Intervention and Geriatrics from the University of Puerto Rico- Medical Science Campus. She went to New York City, and after practicing as an OT in the Manhattan VA Medical Center, she decided to move back to Puerto Rico to become a faculty member of the UPR Humacao OT Department, the place where she has accomplished most of her professional goals.

At Humacao's OT Department, Professor Marrero Díaz has been involved in various educational and administrative duties. She became the first director of the OT Department after the reorganization of the Physical and Occupational Therapy Department. Her contributions as the Occupational Therapy Associate Degree Director have left profound footprints on her students and have had a great impact on the profession. Upon completion of the department director position, she accepted the challenge of establishing a unique OT bachelor program. Professor Marrero Díaz developed and coordinated the accreditation self-study report, the external accreditation, and the state license of this program.

Professor Marrero Díaz has also been the Coordinator for Students Mentoring Program and has been an advisor and active collaborator to the institutional assessment program. She is a member of the Academic Senate and member of the Law and Regulations Committee of this body. At the classroom level, she has conducted research on assessment, which has been presented in professional publications. She has been recognized on various occasions for her pedagogical and administrative performance. The most recent recognition was given by the Puerto Rico OT Association, when she was honored with the Highest Excellence Recognition for her contributions in the profession and for being a role model for her students, co-workers, colleagues, friends, and family.

On a volunteer basis, Professor Marrero Díaz was the Vice President of the OT Examination Board and has been member of the National Roster of Evaluators of the Accreditation Council of OT Education since 2003. She was also President of the Public Relations Committee for the Puerto Rico OT Association, 2007 to 2008.